Explaining Ecosystems

Student Exercises and Teacher Guide for

Grade Ten Academic Science

Mike Lattner   *Algonquin and Lakeshore Catholic District School Board*

Jim Ross   *The University of Western Ontario*

 *London, Ontario Canada*

Authors	Mike Lattner
	Jim Ross
Contributors	
Printer	CreateSpace
Cover Design	Images, London Ontario Canada

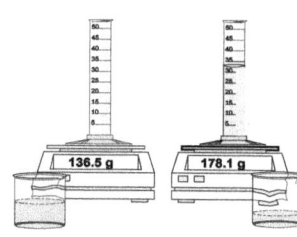

© Copyright 2003 by Ross Lattner Educational Consultants.

All rights reserved. The use of any part of this publication, reproduced, transmitted in any form or by any means, electronic, mechanical, photocopying, recording or otherwise, or stored in a retrieval system, without the prior consent of the publisher, is an infringement of the copyright law and is forbidden.

Permission is granted to the individual teacher who purchases one copy of *Explaining Ecosystems*, to reproduce the student activities for use in his / her classroom only. Reproduction of these materials for an entire school, or for a school system or for other colleagues or for commercial sale is strictly prohibited.

ISBN	978-1-897007-14-3
Offices	London, Ontario Canada

To teachers, parents and students everywhere who desire to bring about new ways of understanding the world.

We welcome your comments and suggestions. Let us know what you find most useful. We've worked hard to remove any errors, but don't let a day go by without letting us know if you find one.

Stay in touch.

Our thanks to all of the wonderful people at the Faculty of Education, the University of Western Ontario.
Special thanks to Jon McGoey, a great biology teacher and a great friend.

Explaining Ecosystems
Table of Contents

Chapter 1: Teacher Guide 1

Activity 1.1: Building Perpetual Motion Machines 4
Activity 1.2: Photosynthesis and Respiration 6
Activity 2.1: Where Does Your Recyclable Material Go? 8
Activity 2.2: A Great Lakes Food Web 10
Activity 2.3: Predators and Prey - A Simulation 12
Activity 2.4: Components of an Ecosystem 14
Activity 2.5: Competition 16
Activity 2.6: Your School Yard - An Ecosystem Out of Balance 18
Lab 3.1: Happiness is a Healthy Local Waterway 20
Lab 3.2: Mercury in Fish and Bioaccumulation 22
Lab 3.3: "There's a Desert in Canada?" - A Look at Canadian Biomes 24
Project 4.1: Energy Technologies 26
Project 4.2: The Case for Vegetarians 28

Explaining Ecosystems
Table of Contents

Chapter 2: Student Exercises 31

Introduction: Biology, Ecosystems and Human Activity 32
Activity 1.1: Building Perpetual Motion Machines 34
Activity 1.2: Photosynthesis and Respiration 36
Activity 2.1: Where Does Your Recyclable Material Go? 38
    The Monetary Value of Recyclable Material 40
    Natural Resources Conserved by Recycling Material 41
Activity 2.2: A Great Lakes Food Web 42
Activity 2.3: Predators and Prey - A Simulation 46
Activity 2.4: Components of an Ecosystem 48
Activity 2.5: Competition 50
Activity 2.6: Your School Yard - An Ecosystem Out of Balance 52
Lab 3.1: Happiness is a Healthy Local Waterway 54
    Abiotic Factors Affecting Aquatic Ecosystems 56
    Habitat Features for Seven Species of Ontario Fish 57
Lab 3.2: Mercury in Fish and Bioaccumulation 58
    Concentration of Mercury in Tissues of Four Species of Great Lakes Fish ... 60
Lab 3.3: "There's a Desert in Canada?" A Look at Canadian Biomes 62
    Characteristics of Canadian Biomes 64
    Climate Data for Twelve Canadian Locations 65
Project 4.1: Energy Technologies 66
Project 4.2: The Case for Vegetarians 68

Appendix: Laboratory Safety 70

Exploring Ecosystems

Chapter 1: Teacher Guide

Title: Explaining Ecosystems

Time Allocation: 27.5 hours (22 periods of 75 minutes each)

Authors: Mike Lattner and Jim Ross

Date: August, 2003

Unit Description: An investigation into environmental sustainability, this unit emphasizes the structures of ecosystems, the cycling of matter and energy within ecosystems, and the ways in which humans affect sustainability of ecosystems. Because this unit involves some outdoor investigations, it should be placed first if taught in the autumn semester, or last, if taught in the winter semester. The unit itself is divided into four sections.

1. The unit begins with a brief consideration of energy and thermodynamics and the limits placed on ecosystems by the first two laws.

2. Recycling matter is the focus of the second part of the unit. Students investigate the water cycle, food webs and other biotic components of ecosystems.

3. Next, students are given the opportunity to investigate abiotic and biotic parameters in a local aquatic ecosystem.

4. The unit concludes with a five-day performance task that will enable students to examine human affects on the sustainability of ecosystems.

Strand: Biology

Expectations: Overall: BEV.01-.03
Specific: BE 1.01-1.07; BE 2.01-.02; BE 3.01-.07

Introduction

10 Academic Science Teacher Guide

It is not difficult for students to grasp the general notion that species depend on one another and on the environment for survival.

Students' awareness of nature must be supported by knowledge of:

1. the kinds of relationships that exist among organisms,

2. the kinds of physical conditions that organisms must cope with,

3. the kinds of environments created by the interaction of organisms with one another and their physical surroundings, and

4. the complexity of ecosystems.

Unit Planning Notes: This unit is intended to provide students with a background in environmental science principles, especially as they relate to the cycling of matter and energy. Since energy is neither created nor destroyed, and since energy is able to be converted from one form into another, but always with a loss during the conversion, ecosystems develop where sustainable energy conversions between living things occur. Similarly, matter must be satisfactorily exchanged among abiotic and biotic components to sustain ecosystems. In this unit, students will be challenged to investigate how matter and energy cycling is sustained in ecosystems. The approach will be to emphasize the explanatory and predictive roles of science, ahead of the empirical. The lab exercises are not designed to provide definitive, once-and-for-all answers to highly refined questions. But rather, the lab exercises are intended to provoke student prediction, and subsequent explanation of selected phenomena.

Prior Knowledge Required: We assume that students are at least familiar with simple relationships among species in ecosystems, *e.g.*, predators and prey, and that an element of balance or fine-tuning exists among the components of ecosystems. Because of the emphasis upon explanation, in this unit we expect that students are capable of writing coherent sentences and paragraphs.

Teaching and Learning Strategies: Our focus in teaching science should be to encourage students to take their everyday thinking to a higher level - a level involving prediction and explanation of natural events. Accordingly, three learning strategies are emphasized. Students are expected to commit to a prediction of the role of an ecosystem component in a natural event for each lab or activity. Students are expected to explain why they believe their prediction, in both diagrammatic representations and in sentences. Finally, students are expected to gradually master a small set of theoretical propositions or facts, and then to increasingly represent their arguments in terms of theory.

Assessment and Evaluation
A variety of strategies and instruments will be used throughout this document. Encourage your students to check the appropriate section of the Knowledge, Inquiry, Communications, Applications (KICA) wheel found at the top of the second page of most lab activities, in accordance with the suggestions given in the Teacher Guide.

Introduction

Science and Pedagogy

The amount of life any ecosystem can support is limited by the available energy and nutrients, and by the ability of ecosystems to recycle the organic materials. Human activities and technologies can have a profound effect on the recycling ability of ecosystems.

The chemical elements that make up organic molecules in living things pass through food webs and are combined and recombined in different ways. At each link in a food web, some energy is stored in newly made structures, but most is dissipated into the environment. Continual input of energy from sunlight keeps the process going.

1. **Thermodynamic Principles**

The universe is made up of just two things: matter and energy. As we learned in Grade 9, matter is what makes up organisms, the food and nutrients that they consume, and the wastes that they produce. Energy is defined as the ability to do work. Energy transformations between **Producers** and **Consumers** play an important role in the functioning of ecosystems.

Organisms use energy to move, perform metabolic functions, and to produce more organisms. All of these energy transformations occur in accordance with **The 1st Law of Thermodynamics**: *Energy is neither created or destroyed, but is converted from one form to another.*

Unfortunately for us, energy transformations are never 100% efficient - there is always loss - usually some energy ends up as heat. Heat energy is less ordered, that is, more random than other higher quality forms of energy. Heat is lower quality energy because it is less able to do useful work. The principle which underlies the loss of heat during energy transformations is referred to as **The 2nd Law of Thermodynamics**, which states: *each time energy is converted into another form, some of that energy is degraded into a lower quality form.*

2. **Energy Transfer and Matter Cycling in Ecosystems**

All organic molecules that make up the tissues of living organisms are highly ordered and contain high potential energy. Living organisms obtain their energy either by consuming or by producing high energy organic molecules. Producers, plants and their aquatic counterparts Cyanobacteria and Algae, are able to produce high energy molecules from carbon dioxide and light energy from the sun. Consumers eat plants or other consumers that ate plants to obtain matter and energy.

The movement of matter and energy among components of ecosystems accounts for the variety of relationships and organisms that exist. When matter is cycled in ecosystems, there is no loss, in accordance with the **Law of Conservation of Mass**, which was part of the Grade 9 curriculum. However, as we learned above, in any energy transfer there is always a loss of energy. In fact, most energy, approximately 90%, is lost in the transfer between feeding or trophic levels. This energy loss will have profound effects on food chains and webs.

10 Applied Science Teacher Guide

Exploring Ecosystems

The 1st Law of Thermodynamics ... Although energy can be changed from one form to another, it can not be created or destroyed.

Activity 1.1: Building Perpetual Motion

Learning Expectations BE1.01: Describe the process of photosynthesis and cellular respiration as they relate to the cycling of energy.

Connections:

        Sciencepower 10: pp. 8 - 9
        Science 10: pp. 36 - 37
Science 10 Concepts and Connections: pp. 22 - 25

Pedagogical Issues

Toys are also readily available and students obviously associate them with fun. In this activity, your job is to try to get students to investigate energy transfers in wind-up toys and to discover why they are never completely efficient. Children naturally want simple explanations, but the energy transfers involved in toys can be complex. For example, it is easy to predict that a wind-up toy will not work indefinitely because of friction. However, you will need to encourage your students to dig a little more deeply into what energy transformations combine to produce the friction. Encourage your students to focus on several events which tend to rob the toy of energy.

The 2nd Law of Thermodynamics ... During any energy conversion, some energy is lost from the system, usually as thermal energy (heat).

The reasons for our emphasis on thermodynamics are twofold:
1) Ecosystems lose energy at every trophic level, therefore, a great deal of energy is lost.
2) Without the constant input of energy from the sun, life on Earth would not be possible.

Science Issues

Some toys are excellent examples of energy conversion machines. A wind-up toy, for example, stores chemical energy from your muscles in the form of elastic potential energy in a spring or elastic band. When turned on, the toy converts this potential energy into kinetic energy as it moves. Heat is produced by the friction between moving parts and contact with air molecules or the molecules on the surface of a floor or table.

Of the solar energy that actually strikes Earth, less than one percent is stored in the chemical energy of plants as a result of photosynthesis.

Energy Flow in Ecosystems

Science and Pedagogy

A wind-up propellor airplane is a great example to use for this lab. By changing the number of windings, the plane will stay aloft for varying amounts of time.

The Learning Activity
Introduce the topic of energy as the chief limiting abiotic factor in ecosystems during a discussion of factors that your students think are important in limiting numbers of organisms. Students will be aware that animals eat plants and that plants get their energy from the sun. Challenge your students to consider what would happen if the sun's energy was blocked from Earth. How long would ecosystems continue to transfer energy? Are there ways to increase the time that energy transfers continue to occur, *i.e.,* ways to conserve energy. With this in mind, demonstrate how a toy airplane, for example, can be adjusted to store energy and to later release it.

Before the experiment, students will:
  Predict: how long will a wind-up toy operate?
  Explain: the prediction, using their own experiences.
  Make sure this explanation is more than a single sentence.

This activity is designed to be a fun activity in which you show that science is fun and involves making and explaining predictions and modifying initial beliefs when faced with more 'scientific' ideas

Allow students to attempt the experiment several times, tweaking the toy each time to enhance performance.

After the experiment, students will:
  Observe: their results and record them in the Lab Manual.
  Explain: their observations with reference to the Laws of Thermodynamics.

Conclude the activity with a discussion of the energy transfers involved. You may want to assign homework to reinforce the concepts discussed in class.

Equipment, Preparation and Resources
Each pair of students should have access to a wind-up toy. Suitable examples are wind-up airplanes, wind-up cars, yo-yo, etc. If you have a collection of toys, then you will always have a way to use spare time (if such a thing exists) in class.

Categories:
Knowledge:
Inquiry:
Communication:
Applications, Extensions:

Assessment and Evaluation
Quality of answers to *Questions for Later ...*
Insight and modifications to toys

Awareness of energy issues in modern society

Ross Lattner Educational Consultants   www.rosslattner.ca

10 Applied Science Teacher Guide

Exploring Ecosystems

Photosynthesis and cellular respiration are essentially reverse processes. The reactants of one process are the products of the other.

Activity 1.2: Photosynthesis and Respiration

Learning Expectations BE 1.01, 2.01: Describe the process of photosynthesis and cellular respiration as they relate to the cycling of energy, carbon and oxygen through biotic and abiotic components of ecosystems; formulate scientific questions about observed ecological relationships.

Connections: Sciencepower 10: pp. 4 - 8; 43, 46 - 47
Science 10: pp. 32 - 35
Science 10 Concepts and Connections: pp. 26 - 29

Pedagogical Issues

Secondary school science students should have sufficient grasp of atoms and molecules to link the conservation of matter with the flow of energy in living systems. Energy can be accounted for by thinking of it as being stored molecular configurations constituted during photosynthesis and released during oxidation. Although there is no need to make a detailed account of all the energy, students should be aware of heat generated by consumers and decomposers in their life functions.

At times, environmental conditions are such that plants and marine organisms grow faster than decomposers can recycle them back to the environment. Layers of energy-rich organic material have been gradually turned into great coal beds and oil pools by the pressure of the overlying earth. By burning these fossil fuels, people are passing most of the stored energy back into the environment as heat and releasing large amounts of carbon dioxide.

Science Issues

Food provides the fuel and the building material for all organisms. Plants use the energy from light to make sugars from carbon dioxide and water. This food can be used immediately or stored for later use. Consumers break down plant structures to produce the materials and energy they need to survive. Animals that are eaten by other organisms pass on their energy and matter to higher order consumers.

In grade 9, students were introduced to chemical tests for gases. Students observed that limewater turns milky in the presence of carbon dioxide, in accordance with the following reaction: $CO_2 + Ca(OH)_2$ (in limewater) → $CaCO_3 + H_2O$. In addition, students observed that oxygen gas rekindles a glowing wooden splint. Both of these tests are repeated in this activity. To prepare limewater, make a saturated solution of $Ca(OH)_2$ then filter or allow the mixture to settle overnight and decant the supernatant. You can extend the investigation by asking students to record the amount of time necessary to turn limewater milky when they exhale before and after some strenuous exercise.

Energy Flow in Ecosystems

Science and Pedagogy

The Learning Activity

In this simple investigation, student determine the presence of carbon dioxide in their exhaled air. The teacher demonstration is to test for the presence of oxygen using a glowing splint.

Before the experiment, students will:
 Predict: the identity of the gas, based on experience.
 Explain: the prediction using sentences.

After the experiment, students will
 Observe: the results of the chemical tests for each gas.
 Explain: the observations using chemical equations for cellular respiration and photosynthesis.

Remind students to look for energy transformations involved in each chemical process. Cellular respiration involves energy released (some as heat) from food. Photosynthesis requires solar energy, however, some is dispersed as the green light reflected

It is relatively easy to maintain a culture of aquatic plants in you science lab. Collect *Elodea* (water weed) from a lake or pond in a large jar during summer or save student model ecosystems (Activity 3.8 in the Lab Manual) from year to year.

Collect oxygen from aquatic plants using a large glass funnel inverted over a beaker containing *Elodea* in bright sunlight. However, it is difficult to collect enough gas to test quickly. You can (enhance) the amount if you collect oxygen from an electrolysis apparatus prior to class and store it in a sealed test tube for the later test.

Equipment, Preparation and Resources (class of 24)
- 12 Erlenmeyer flasks
- 12 test tubes
- large glass funnel
- culture of *Elodea sp.* (water weed)
- electrolysis apparatus (optional)
- 12 straws
- 1 L of lime water
- wooden splints

Categories:
Knowledge:
Inquiry:
Communication:
Applications, Extensions:

Assessment and Evaluation
Quality of explanation of observations
Correctly interprets results of chemical tests (optional)

Ross Lattner Educational Consultants www.rosslattner.ca

Exploring Ecosystems

10 Applied Science Teacher Guide

More than 75 % of municipal solid waste is recyclable.

Some impediments to instituting recycling programs:

reluctance to sort

lack of standards in sorted and non-sorted materials

lack of reprocessing facilities

insufficient marketing of recycled materials

vested interest in maintaining the status quo

Activity 2.1: Where Does Your Recyclable

Learning Expectations BE 1.02, 2.01: Illustrate the cycling of matter through biotic and abiotic components of an ecosystem; analyze data and information gathered to clarify aspects of the concern or issue.

Connections: Sciencepower 10: N/A
Science 10: N/A
Science 10 Concepts and Connections: N/A

Pedagogical Issues

Students learning about matter and energy cycling in ecosystems can begin to think that they are separate from these processes if no practical connection is identified. Therefore, it is important to link student consumption with their use and cycling of matter derived from natural resources. Emphasize how matter bound in durable items, like pop cans, glass bottles, cardboard packaging, etc., must be returned to the environment by some means. Of course, the best way to avoid waste management problems is to reduce consumption or to reuse that which has already been produced. However, recycling (primarily accomplished by means of Blue Boxes) will ultimately reduce the environmental impact of humans.

Science Issues

One of the principles involved in maintaining sustainable ecosystems is ensuring that all matter in nutrients and wastes are recycled. In contrast to this principle, modern society has been based primarily on a uni-directional flow of elements. For example, nutrients bound in forest products are obtained in one location but used in others. The same can be said for agriculture, mining, and commercial fishing. This one-way flow leads to at least two problems: depletion of the resource at one location, and pollution at the other. Aggravating these problems is the fact that many of the products we consume are produced from synthetic organic compounds, such as plastics, that are not biodegradable. Hence, naturally occurring organisms such as bacteria, fungi, and insects cannot break down these compounds into their constituent elements.

Cycling Matter in Ecosystems

Science and Pedagogy

Reprocessing options for recycled goods:

paper can be re-pulped and reprocessed into recycled paper and other paper products

glass can be crushed, remelted, and made into new containers or used as a substitute for gravel or sand in concrete or asphalt

metals can be remelted and re-fabricated (making aluminum from scrap aluminum saves up to 90% of the energy required to make aluminum from ore)

textiles can be shredded and used to strengthen recycled paper products

The Learning Activity

In this activity, students look at their family's use and consumption of natural resources. Each student must make a record of the packaging, glass, *etc.* that they use in a week. This data is then pooled with class data.

Remind your students to start looking for recycling information in advance of today's class. It will be very important for students to be able to speak confidently about their family's consumption and production of recyclable material. In the absence of actual data, students will have to estimate.

Before the experiment, students will:
Predict: the amount of material that your class could have recycled this week.
Explain: how this prediction, or estimate is imperfect, but a reasonable first step in determining the amount of material recycled.

In their Lab Manuals, students will record their family data and make calculations of the amount of mass, energy, and money that the entire class could save by recycling.

After the experiment, students will
Observe: the amount of matter, energy, and money saved by recycling.
Explain: the value of recycling with reference to money, matter, and energy.

Following the activity, students will answer the questions for later in the Lab Manual.

Equipment, Preparation and Resources (class of 24)
- Lab Manual
- Calculator

Categories: **Assessment and Evaluation**
Knowledge: Quality of responses to *Questions for Later ...*
Inquiry:
Communication:
Applications, Extensions: Recognition of societal implications of recycling waste

10 Applied Science Teacher Guide

Exploring Ecosystems

For sustainability, the size of consumer populations must be maintained such that over consumption of prey species does not occur.

Activity 2.2: A Great Lakes Food Web

Learning Expectations BE 1.04: Show the relationship between the resources available and the equilibrium of a natural population in an ecosystem.

Connections: Sciencepower 10: pp. 8 - 17
Science 10: pp. 10 - 11; 34, 54
Science 10 Concepts and Connections: pp. 22 - 25

Pedagogical Issues

Students need to build up a collection of cases, based on their own experience, studies of organisms, readings, and video presentations, of the kinds of interactions that take place between organisms. To facilitate this edification process, teachers should try to integrate students' existing knowledge with many examples. This activity is based on an aquatic food web; many of your students will have very limited knowledge of aquatic organisms.

Pyramids of energy, biomass, and numbers help reinforce the notion that producers and lower-order consumers support the rest of the organisms in an ecosystem.

The concept of an ecosystem should bring coherence to the complex inter-relationships among organisms and environments. Students' understanding can be enhanced by reinforcement of the inter-dependence of organisms based on their feeding relationships.

Science Issues

Two types of organisms may interact with one another in several ways: they may be in a producer / consumer, predator / prey, or parasite / host relationship. In addition, one organism may scavenge or decompose the other. These relationships may be competitive or mutually beneficial. Some species have become so adapted to each other that neither could survive without the other.

The top carnivore in many Great Lakes ecosystems was once the Atlantic salmon. However, many changes in the lakes has resulted in a near total loss in this predatory fish. Restocking of this species still occurs to at least some degree by American efforts to establish a put-and-take fishery.

Aquatic ecosystems can be quite complex as many individuals and organisms inhabit essentially the same space (*i.e.,* water), but use and partition resources with a bewildering degree of diversity. The information page, found with the activity in the Lab Manual contains all of the information necessary for students to build their understanding of the inter-relationships among aquatic organisms.

Cycling Matter in Ecosystems

Science and Pedagogy

A Great Lakes Food Chain

(Top carnivore) osprey
⇑
(3° consumer) walleye
⇑
(2° consumer) perch
⇑
(1° consumer) mayfly larva
⇑
(Producer) phytoplankton

The Learning Activity

In this activity, students put together a number of ideas surrounding the notion of stability in food webs. Begin with a brief explanation of the terms: predator and prey, and a review of the terms: consumer, producer, and trophic level. Then invite students to come up with examples of organisms within a terrestrial ecosystem. Next, extend the discussion to include aquatic organisms that students may have encountered while fishing, while visiting cottages, *etc.*, or from television. Then, introduce the activity and allow students to build their own ideas about the feeding relationships that exist among organisms. Insist that students prepare their pyramids of biomass and food webs after discussing each of the four food webs in the Lab Manual with a friend or partner.

Homework could be assigned to reinforce the concept of feeding relationships among organisms in a ecosystem.

Biomass at successive trophic levels:

1 kg osprey
⇑
10 kg walleye
⇑
100 kg perch
⇑
1000 kg mayfly nymphs
⇑
10 000 kg phytoplankton

Equipment, Preparation and Resources (class of 24)
Lab Manuals
Graph paper (optional)

Categories:
Knowledge:
Inquiry:
Communication:
Applications, Extensions:

Assessment and Evaluation
Quality of response to *Questions for Later ...*

Quality of diagram of food web and biomass pyramid

10 Applied Science Teacher Guide

Exploring Ecosystems

A stable population in nature is the result of a balance between factors that tend to increase population, also known as biotic potential, and factors tending to decrease numbers - environmental resistance.

Activity 2.3: Predators and Prey - A

Learning Expectations BE 1.04; 1.06: Show the relationship between the resources available and the equilibrium of a natural population in an ecosystem.; describe how different ecosystems respond differently to short-term stresses and long-term changes.

Connections: Sciencepower 10: pp. 18 - 20
Science 10: pp. 20 - 21
Science 10 Concepts and Connections: pp. 38 - 41

Biotic Potential
- reproductive rate
- ability to migrate
- ability to disperse seeds
- defense mechanisms
- ability to tolerate harsh conditions

Pedagogical Issues
Stability and change in ecosystems will be considered in this activity with reference to the population size of a predator - lynx (*Lynx canadensis*) and its chief prey species - snowshoe hare (*Lepus americanus*). This classic example of predator-prey relationships, based on data collected in Canada from 1850 to 1930, has been used to demonstrate the regular fluctuation that occurs in population density of both animal species. Although our focus will be on one mechanism of population control, make your students aware that in natural ecosystems, all mechanisms are working at once to create an overall balance.

Science Issues
Ecosystems can be reasonably stable over hundreds or thousands of years. As any population of organisms grows, it is held in check by one or more environmental factors: depletion of food or breeding sites, and higher losses due to increased rates of predation or parasitism.

Like many complex systems, ecosystems tend to have cyclic fluctuations around a state of rough equilibrium. However, over an extended period, ecosystems always change when climate changes or when one or more new species appear as a result of migration or local evolution.

We are part of Earth's ecosystems. Human activities can, deliberately or inadvertently, alter the equilibrium in ecosystems.

Environmental Resistance
- lack of food or nutrients
- lack of water
- lack of suitable habitat
- adverse weather conditions
- predators
- disease
- parasites
- competition

Cycling Matter in Ecosystems

Science and Pedagogy

Hare and lynx numbers (x 1000), based on pelts received by Hudson's Bay Company

Year	Hare	Lynx
1850	38.5	0.95
1852	60.5	0.55
1854	91.2	1.25
1856	62.5	2.85
1858	15.2	1.45
1860	28.4	0.33
1862	4.5	0.32
1864	144	3.04
1866	62.4	5.91
1868	5.2	1.10
1870	9.5	0.86
1872	24.5	0.37
1874	48.5	2.65
1876	89.4	4.25
1878	40.2	2.80
1880	6.5	0.76
1882	7.7	1.15
1884	47.5	4.35
1886	131	6.33
1888	17.5	2.68
1890	24.5	1.05
1892	41.2	1.25
1894	76.4	3.10
1896	82.5	4.85
1898	3.5	0.45
1900	10.1	0.31

The Learning Activity Introduce this activity with a brief description of lynx and hare and the fact that scientific data can be collected in a variety of ways (*i.e.,* from trappers). Lynx and hare numbers show regular fluctuations of great magnitude. Each cycle lasts approximately 10 years and cycles of the two species are highly synchronized, with peaks in lynx abundance tending to trail those in hare by a year or two.

Before the experiment, students will:
  Predict: what will happen to the number of predators in an ecosystem if the numbers of its principal prey increase.
  Explain: why this will happen and whether or not there will be any time delay in peak numbers.

Using the numbers at left, and following instructions in the Lab Manual, students will make a detailed graph of lynx and hare numbers.

After the experiment, students will
  Observe: the time delay between peaks in the abundance of hare and lynx.
  Explain: this time delay with reference to biotic potential and environmental resistance in populations.

Students will complete the *Questions for Later ...* as a homework assignment.

Conclude the lesson with a brief discussion of the value of diversity in food webs. For example, if a predator is able to eat many different species, it may support itself in times when its preferred prey is at low density. This will tend to reduce the time delay between peaks in the prey and predator population.

Equipment, Preparation and Resources (class of 24)
Lab Manual
Graph paper
Coloured pencils

Categories:	Assessment and Evaluation
Knowledge / Understanding:	Answer to *Questions for Later ...*
Inquiry:	Demonstrates skills in graphing and interpreting graph
Communication:	
Making	Links diversity of ecosystem with stability and sustainability

10 Applied Science Teacher Guide

Exploring Ecosystems

Students will need to consider the following cycles when they design their ecosystems:

Oxygen
Carbon
Nitrogen
Phosphorus
Sulfur
Water

Some essential components of a model ecosystem:
Producers
Consumer
Decomposer / Scavenger
Water

Activity 2.4: Components of an Ecosystem

Learning Expectations BE 1.01; .02; .04; .06-.07: Describe the processes of photosynthesis and cellular respiration as they relate to the cycling of energy, carbon, and oxygen through abiotic and biotic components of an ecosystem; show the relationship between the resources available and the equilibrium of a natural population in an ecosystem; describe how different ecosystems respond differently to short-term stresses and long-term changes; explain how soil composition and fertility can be altered in an ecosystem and outline the possible consequences of such changes.

Connections: Sciencepower 10: pp. 38 - 39
Science 10: pp. 60 - 61
Science 10 Concepts and Connections: pp. 22 - 23

Pedagogical Issues

Organisms are linked to one another and to their physical setting by the transfer and transformation of matter and energy. This fundamental concept brings together insights from the physical and biological sciences. However, energy transfer in biological systems is less obvious than in physical systems. In this activity students will attempt to produce a sustaining ecosystem in a jar. Once established, the amount of matter contained within the jar is fixed. External energy will be supplied largely by natural sunlight. The amount of time that this model ecosystem functions will be a consequence of the planning and achievement of students.

Science Issues

Organisms take substances from the non-living environment and, in turn, they return substances into the water, soil and air. In natural ecosystems, these interactions are more or less balanced. The success of the model ecosystems that your students produce will be dependent largely on the balance and care they demonstrate when establishing their model ecosystems. Model ecosystems can be established in test tubes prior to this class. Add a health sprig of *Elodea* and a snail such as *Physa.* Seal the test tube with a stopper and tape. Several different test tubes, each containing different components can be used to demonstrate what happens when, for example, snails are omitted from the model. A dilute indicator of brom thymol blue can be used to indicate the presence of CO_2. Exhale into a quantity of dilute brom thymol blue until it is just at its turning point to yellow before adding it to the test tube.

Cycling Matter in Ecosystems

Science and Pedagogy

The Learning Activity

This activity should be set up during the first two days of this strand and then students can observe their model over the course of the Ecosystems unit.

Before the experiment, students will:
Predict: how long you will be able to keep the fish alive without removing the lid, or changing the model ecosystem in any way.
Explain: what role is played by each of the components of the model ecosystem in cycling matter and sustaining conditions for life.

The models should be stored in the science lab during the entire unit of study. Students should make regular observations.

After the experiment, students will
Observe: the activities of the ecosystem over the course of your investigation, noting any changes in appearance and when they occurred.
Explain: the changes that occurred with reference to interruptions in cycling of matter and energy.

Equipment, Preparation and Resources (class of 24)
Students will need to supply their own jars
- test tubes (optional)

Assessment and Evaluation

Categories:	
Knowledge:	Answers to *Questions for Later* ...
Inquiry:	Quality of observations
Communication:	Clarity of answers and any drawings
Applications, Extensions:	Recognizes model components mimic natural ecosystems

10 Applied Science Teacher Guide

Exploring Ecosystems

In crowded populations, plants suffer high mortality, slowed growth, and reduced ability to reproduce.

Activity 2.5: Competition

Learning Expectations BE 1.04; 2.01: Show the relationship between the resources available and the equilibrium of a natural population in an ecosystem; demonstrate the skills required to plan and conduct an inquiry into ecological relationships, using instruments, apparatus, and materials safely and accurately.

Connections: Sciencepower 10: pp. 18 - 20
   Science 10: pp. 17, 41
Science 10 Concepts and Connections: pp. 38 - 41

Pedagogical Issues

The concept of competition, both interspecific - between individuals in different species, and intraspecific - among individuals within a single species, is an important prerequisite concept to a later understanding of natural selection. In this activity students are exposed to both types of competition. Our focus is to engage students to think about limited resources and to observe the results of intense competition evident in reduced growth.

Darwin remarked in the Origin of Species "As species of the same genus have usually, though by no means invariably, some similarity in habits and constitution, and always in structure, the struggle will generally be more severe between species of the same genus, when they come into competition with each other, than between species of distinct genera". Darwin reasoned that similar structure indicated similar ecology, especially resource requirements.

Science Issues

In all environments - freshwater, marine, forest, desert, grassland, mountain, and others - organisms with similar needs may compete with one another for limited resources, including food, space, water, air, and shelter. Often intraspecific competition is greatest since these individuals have the most similar life requirements.

Spinach, although it will grow almost anywhere, likes cool conditions best. Its seeds germinate very slowly, but once above the soil, the plants grow rapidly. Spinach owes its deep green colour to a high nitrogen content. This activity could be extended to consider the effect of additional high-nitrogen fertilizer on competition.

Corn grows best in high temperature with lots of fertilizer.

Ross Lattner Educational Consultants   www.rosslattner.ca

Cycling Matter in Ecosystems

Science and Pedagogy

There appear to be ongoing difficulties in addressing the learning needs of the typical child in an applied level course. How many of these difficulties arise from a lack of clear direction in our pedagogy?

A common mistake, not limited to pedagogy, is to create a false distinction between "theory" and "practice." In the classroom, this mistake has set up a dichotomy between the "academic" class and the "applied" class. This dichotomy costs both groups.

Students in the academic course receive an emphasis upon conceptual and formal procedural knowledge, often at the expense of practical experiences. As their knowledge becomes increasingly distanced from meaningful personal experience, it frequently becomes narrower and more formal as well.

The Learning Activity

Set up this activity during the first two days of the unit (or earlier if possible). Students need to observe differential growth rates as evidence of the competition for limited resources.

Before the experiment, students will:
Predict: which container will support the greatest growth.
Explain: the prediction with reference to the competition for resources by individuals within and between species.

After about three weeks, students will
Observe: the appearance of each container and determine the average mass of a corn and a spinach plant in each container with an electronic balance. Students should be encouraged to share their data.
Explain: the results with reference to average growth rate of plants and magnitude, and type of competition.

This period could be used to mass all of the plants, perform calculations, and then to clean up.

Equipment, Preparation and Resources (class of 24)

- 60 small containers or plant pots
- 4 L or more of potting soil
- 144 spinach, and corn seeds
- space and light to grow plants
- watering containers

Although a window sill could be adequate for this activity if you have a small class, access to a green house would be very useful. The important thing to maintain is similar growing conditions for all of the plants

Categories:
Knowledge:
Inquiry:
Communication:
Applications, Extensions:

Assessment and Evaluation
Quality of explanations and responses to *Questions for Later ...*
Use of equipment; accuracy of measurements

Exploring Ecosystems

Activity 2.6: Your School Yard -
An Ecosystem Out of Balance

Learning Expectations BE 1.02;.07;.08; 3.01:
Illustrate the cycling of matter through an ecosystem by tracking nitrogen; compare a natural and disturbed ecosystem and suggest ways to assuring their sustainability; explain how soil composition and fertility can be altered in an ecosystem and outline the possible consequences of such changes; assess the impact of technological change and natural change on an ecosystem.

Pedagogical Issues
Students generally respond well to case studies, in that they can examine real-world issues in light of their in-school learning. The effect of human imposed environmental change is the focus of this study. Your job in this study is not so much to provide students with the "right" answers about human actions, but rather, to see to it that students know what questions to ask. This activity should provide students with the opportunity to add detail to their awareness of the effects of human presence on life. For example, the deliberate planting of lawns and gardens, including foreign species, has changed ecosystems. Out of this we hope will come an awareness that people can make some decisions about what life on Earth will survive and a sense of responsibility about exercising power.

Science Issues
Many issues are packed into this study - nutrient cycling, energy concerns, introduction of foreign species, soil compaction, and the use of herbicides and pesticides will be investigated. In general, human alteration of the environment results in the loss of habitats by loss of biodiversity. Human use of habitats often simplifies natural ecosystems. For example, in school yards we remove fallen trees, we plant shrubs and annual flowers in neat rows, we apply artificial fertilizer and herbicides. In addition, we interfere with cycling of matter and energy in numerous ways - *e.g.*, watering lawns, removing lawn waste, adding artificial fertilizers, and compacting soil.

Effects of Maintaining Large Lawns on Matter and Energy Cycling

• Water Cycle - increased runoff, decreased filtration, flooding, increased evaporation due to use of lawn sprinklers

• Nitrogen Cycle - artificial fertilizer, failure to compost results in exporting nutrients, use of herbicides to prevent growth of clover and other legumes

• Carbon Cycle - artificial fertilizers requires use of fossil fuels and lots of energy to produce it, failure to compost results in exporting nutrients

• Sulfur and Phosphorus Cycles - artificial fertilizer, failure to compost results in exporting nutrients

Cycling Matter in Ecosystems

Science and Pedagogy

... Continued

Students in the "applied" courses are expected to make sets of practical decisions, often in the absence of appropriate instruction in theory. This often leaves them with an even greater learning task than the kids in the "academic" class. Not only are they expected to make complex decisions, but they are expected to simply pick up the necessary theory out of thin air.

In the classroom, *Theory* and *Practice* must be first united, and then balanced. When a student makes a practical judgement, he or she uses some kind of theory to do so. That theory is likely inadequate, unarticulated and unscientific. If we expect kids in applied science classes to make scientific judgements about the world around them, we must take seriously their need for theoretical understanding.

Their need may require meaning and experience before words and definitions.

The Learning Activity

This activity requires one day in the school yard and one day to investigate uses of pesticides, herbicides, fertilizers, and what is done with lawn and garden wastes. Prior to the investigation, speak to your Principal and custodial staff and find out what arrangements are currently in place for lawn and garden maintenance. Based on that information, you should be able to assist your students and answer their questions.

Before the experiment, students will:
  Predict: the effects of maintaining their school yard on the natural cycling of matter and energy
  Explain: how each of the nutrient cycles is somehow affected.

Students should be guided through a systematic investigation of the activities and financial resources used to maintain the school yard. It would be great to have custodial staff on hand to answer questions, but not to pass on any judgements about environmental issues. Let the students come to their own conclusions.

After the experiment, students will
  Observe: the effects of school yard maintenance on energy and matter cycles and record these in the space provided in the Lab Manual.
  Explain: these effects using sentences and diagrams of nutrient cycles where appropriate.

Peer tutors could assist with crowd control. Invite your Principal to help answer questions about school and school board policies related to school yard maintenance (and to give them a chance to get out of their office).

Equipment, Preparation and Resources (class of 24)
Information on lawn and garden maintenance at your school
Lab Manual

Categories:	Assessment and Evaluation
Knowledge:	Quality of explanations and answers to *Questions for Later ...*
Inquiry:	
Communication:	Skills used to dig up answers to tough questions
Applications, Extensions:	Clarity and coherence of explanations

10 Applied Science Teacher Guide

Exploring Ecosystems

The main chemical components of aquatic ecosystems studied in this investigation are:

pH
Temperature
Dissolved Oxygen
Alkalinity
Phosphates
Chlorides
Ammonia
Nitrates

Sources of pollutants found in water systems:

nutrients from lawn and garden fertilizer (ammonia, nitrates and phosphates)

insecticides and herbicides used on lawns and gardens

bacteria from fecal wastes of pets (decomposition results in decrease in dissolved oxygen)

road salt (chlorides)

oil and grease picked up from road surfaces or disposed of in storm drains

Lab 3.1: Happiness is a Healthy Local

Learning Expectations BE 2.02; 3.01: Compile data on the biodiversity within a natural ecosystem, using appropriate techniques, and compare the results with those from a disturbed ecosystem; assess the impact of technological change on an ecosystem.

Connections: Sciencepower 10: pp. 11 - 13
Science 10: pp. 143 - 145
Science 10 Concepts and Connections: pp. 20 - 21

Pedagogical Issues

Students should be given an opportunity to explore and investigate natural ecosystems to gain a sense of their complexity. On paper, ecosystems can be easily lumped into arbitrary categories and studied in isolation. In the field, the vast dimensions, and apparent diversity brings to students a sense of wonder at the diversity of life.

Measuring such abiotic factors as pH and alkalinity is an entry point into conditions that affect aquatic ecosystems, and by extension, biomes and the rest of the biosphere. Students can be made aware of how humans affect abiotic factors only after witnessing first-hand, conditions in a natural setting.

Science Issues

The chemical factors selected for study are those most often considered by federal and provincial biologists investigating stream ecology. The abiotic components of aquatic ecosystems, especially, pH, temperature, oxygen and alkalinity, play a crucial role in determining the fish species identified, which are indicator species of the composition of other biotic components, perhaps more so than in terrestrial ecosystems. In addition, these chemical components are relatively easy to measure and can be compared to other bodies of water.

Water chemistry kits are available from a number of biological suppliers. Most come with relatively simple instructions and tips on sampling technique. Although accuracy in sampling is important, the more fundamental issue, we believe, is to get students out into the field.

Abiotic and Biotic Factors

Science and Pedagogy

The habitat preferences of these seven species of Ontario fish is presented in the Lab Manual:

rainbow trout
walleye
smallmouth bass
yellow perch
crappie
carp
catfish

The Learning Activity

This activity is a field investigation that will require approximately ½ day. In addition, time will be necessary to plan in advance which students will be collecting what data. Arrange to have peer tutors or other senior students available to help you maintain crowd control.

Select a nearby stream, pond, or lake that you or someone on your staff knows something about. Almost any waterway will be satisfactory; as long as access to public land (or a friend) is available. Arrange transportation, and any necessary permission.

Before the field investigation, students will:
Predict: the species of fish that they expect to find in the waterway.
Explain: why the student believes the conditions of this waterway are suitable for these species to survive.

Collect data on the eight chemical factors identified in the Lab Manual, the types of fish observed, or known to exist in the waterway, and any other features that you think are valuable. Some other important factors are:
1. Size of the pebbles/ stones on the bottom of streams
2. Types and numbers of insects on the bottom of the waterway
3. Features of vegetation surrounding the waterway, *e.g.,* trees covering the water, shrubs along the shore, *etc.*

During the field investigation, students will
Observe: the features of the waterway as instructed, then
Explain: using your observations and the data collected, why this waterway is able to support the species it does.

Equipment, Preparation and Resources (class of 24)
- 8 water chemistry sampling kits (including pH, alkalinity, nitrates, ammonia, chlorides, phosphates, and dissolved oxygen)
- thermometers

Assessment and Evaluation

Categories:
Knowledge: Quality of explanations and answers to *Questions for Later ...*
Inquiry: Skills demonstrated in using water chemistry kits to obtain data
Communication: Clarity and coherence of explanations
Applications, Extensions: Ability to link observed stream conditions with human activities

The trait that makes heavy metals and nonbiodegradable synthetic organics particularly hazardous is their tendency to accumulate in primarily, the fatty tissues of organisms. Because of bioaccumulation, small, seemingly harmless amounts received over a long period of time may reach toxic levels.

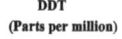
DDT
(Parts per million)

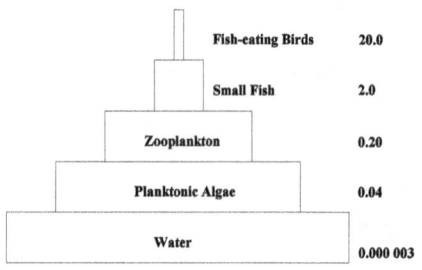

Lab 3.2: Mercury in Fish and Bioaccumulation

Learning Expectations BE1.03: Illustrate the process of bioaccumulation through an example, and explain its potential impact on the viability and diversity of consumers at all trophic levels.

Connections: Sciencepower 10: pp. 30 - 32
Science 10: pp. 54 - 55
Science 10 Concepts and Connections: pp. 32 - 37

Pedagogical Issues
In this lesson, the concept of conservation of mass is considered in relation to thermodynamics and conservation of energy. Because approximately 90 % of the energy is lost between subsequent trophic levels, organisms must constantly eat to obtain energy necessary for life functions. However, nonbiodegradable matter remains primarily in fatty tissues, once consumed by organisms. Thus, even small, apparently insignificant amounts of potentially toxic material can accumulate, especially in organisms near the top of food chains.

Science Issues
Heavy metals and other nonbiodegradable, primarily synthetic, organic compounds enter the body of organisms dissolved in water. Some heavy metals bind to enzymes and are removed from solution. Synthetic organic compounds (*e.g.*, DDT) are highly soluble in the lipids of cell membranes but only sparingly soluble in water. Thus, traces of heavy metals and synthetic organic compounds that are consumed with food and water are trapped and held by the body's enzymes and lipids, while the water and soluble wastes are passed in urine.

Bioaccumulation, which occurs in individual organisms, is compounded in food chains. Small amounts of toxins found in water, and subsequently planktonic algae, for example, become magnified in zooplankton, small fish, through each trophic level and finally in fish-eating birds. Effectively, all the contaminant accumulated by the large biomass at the bottom of a food pyramid is concentrated, through food chains, into the smaller and smaller biomass of organisms at the top of the pyramid.

Abiotic and Biotic Factors

Science and Pedagogy

The Learning Activity
This is a two-part activity involving both theoretical and practical aspects of bioaccumulation. Students will graph the relationship between mass of fish and concentration of mercury to show a positive, near linear relationship. Next, students will make a standard recipe of Kool-Aid® and then four 10 to 1 dilutions. The expectation is that students will see the difference in colour between less than one part per million and a solution nearly one hundred thousand times more concentrated.

Before the experiment, students will:
Predict: which species of fish will have the highest concentration of mercury.
Explain: your prediction based on size and age of these fish.

Students will then use the data provided in the lab manual
After plotting the data, students will
Observe: the resulting relationship between fish mass and concentration of mercury.
Explain: this relationship based on your understanding of bioaccumulation.

Equipment, Preparation and Resources (class of 24)
- 12 packages (6 g) of grape Kool-Aid®
- 24 beakers (1 L)
- 12 graduated cylinders (100 mL)
- graph paper

Demonstrate to students the technique for the first dilution by pouring the package of Kool-Aid® into a 1 L beaker then adding water to the 1000 mL mark. Pour 100 mL of this solution into another 1000 mL beaker, then add water to the 1000 mL mark.

Categories:	Assessment and Evaluation
Knowledge:	Quality of explanations and answers to *Questions for Later ...*
Inquiry:	Skill in use of equipment
Communication:	Detail evident in the graph, clarity of explanations
Applications, Extensions:	Connects concentration with intensity of colour

Exploring Ecosystems

Lab 3.3: "There's a Desert in Canada?" - A Look at Canadian Biomes

Learning Expectations BE 1.05: Explain why ecosystems with similar characteristics can exist in different geographical locations.

Connections: Sciencepower 10: N/A
Science 10: pp. 88 - 92
Science 10 Concepts and Connections: pp. 42 - 44

Pedagogical Issues

High school students generally do not recognize that biomes reflect the response of different ecosystems to different climate conditions. These biomes are made up of ecosystems that vary greatly in species composition but exhibit common functions such as energy flow and the cycling of matter. This activity is intended to increase students' awareness of the diversity of biomes in Canada and of the biome that was present near their school prior to its construction.

Science Issues

Although the biosphere really is a single unit, it can be useful to focus on smaller portions - biomes, which are based on climate patterns. The range of temperature, length of the growing season, and the amount of precipitation determine which plants can survive in an area. In turn, these plants determine which other organisms will be present. Together, the distinct flora and fauna represent a biome. The distribution of biomes is largely determined by Earth's geology and the patterns of air and water currents.

Within Canada exist tundra, alpine (or mountain), boreal forest, temperate forest, temperate rain forest, grassland, and desert biomes.

Abiotic and Biotic Factors

Science and Pedagogy

The Biomes of Selected Canadian Locations

Location	Biome
Ecum Secum	Boreal forest
Swift Current	Grassland
Spring Island	Coastal rain forest
Ashcroft River	Grassland
Ennadai Lake	Boreal forest
Ethelda Bay	Coastal rain forest
Kamloops	Grassland
Cold Lake	Boreal forest
Chatham	Temperate forest
Goose Bay	Boreal forest
Guelph	Temperate forest
Dryden	Boreal forest

The Learning Activity

This is a paper and pencil exercise which invites students to use data provided about biomes to enable students to place Canadian locations in their appropriate biome.

Before the experiment, students will:
Predict: in what biome is your school situated?
Explain: the prediction based on their current knowledge of ecosystems and their characteristics.

Using data in the Lab Manual, students identify the biomes to which each of the Canadian locations belong.

After the activity, students will
Explain: why they placed each city or location in its particular biome.

Equipment, Preparation and Resources (class of 24)
Lab manual

Categories: Assessment and Evaluation
- Knowledge: Correct choice of biomes based on data
- Inquiry:
- Communication:
- Applications, Extensions: Realizes home location is part of a biome

10 Applied Science Teacher Guide

Exploring Ecosystems

Different ways of obtaining, transforming, and distributing energy have different environmental consequences.

Energy from the sun (and the wind and water energy derived from it) is available indefinitely. Because the flow of energy is weak and variable, very large collection systems are needed. Other sources do not renew, or renew very slowly.

Decisions to slow the depletion of energy sources through efficient technology can be made at many levels, from personal to national, and they always involve trade-offs of economic costs and social values.

Some alternative energy sources:
biomass energy
fuel cell technology
geothermal power
wind power
solar power
photo-voltaic cells
energy from wave and tidal sources

Project 4.1: Energy Technologies

Learning Expectations BE 3.01;.03;.05-.07: Assess the impact of technological change on an ecosystem; identify and research a local issue involving an ecosystem; propose a course of action, taking into account human and environmental needs, and defend their position in oral or written form; identify and evaluate Canadian initiatives in protecting Canadian ecosystems; describe careers that involve knowledge of or environmental technologies.

Connections:
Sciencepower 10 : Chapter 4
Science 10 : p. 39
Science 10 Concepts and Connections: NA

Pedagogical Issues

All sources of energy for home or industrial use are derived from energy conversions. The efficiency of these energy conversions and the concomitant effect these have on the environment in terms of production of waste carbon dioxide, sulfur dioxide, and nitrogen oxides is the focus of this performance task. Students will be asked to investigate alternative energy sources - that is, not generation from hydro-electric, nuclear, or from fossil fuels. In their investigation students should look for economic, social, and environmental impacts of the technology.

Science Issues

Whether it involves communications technology, agriculture, fishing, forestry, mining, manufacturing or virtually every other sector, industrial development makes additional demands for energy. In addition, energy is required to heat or cool homes, preserve food, and to cook meals. As the world population grows, and as countries in the developing world continue to make a transition to an industrial economy, the world's energy demands will increase rapidly. Currently, fossil fuels remain the primary source of energy for industrialized nations. However, there is a finite supply of fossil fuels that is being rapidly depleted. Moreover, extraction, transportation, and combustion of fossil fuels are all environmentally dangerous practices. Future generations cannot rely on fossil fuels as heavily as the current generation. The answer to the world's energy demands undoubtedly lies in development of alternative energy sources.

Research Project

Science and Pedagogy

Some starting points for Internet research:

www.sunpower.linkopp.net
Madoc, ON source for solar power and alternative energy resources

www,oee.nrcan.gc.ca/english/programs/index.cfm
Natural Resources Canada Office of Energy Efficiency

www.crest.org/index.html
United States Center for Renewable Energy and Sustainable Technology

www.altenergyresources.com
Cambridge, ON source of alternative energy resources

www.sunwindwater.com/
Northern Ontario source for alternate energy products

The Learning Activity

Over a period of five days, students choose an alternative energy source to investigate. Each student will prepare a report on at least one energy technology involving a Canadian initiative. The report should be approximately five double-spaced pages and include relevant diagrams along with explanation.

Day 1 Students will choose an alternative energy technology to study. It must involve a Canadian initiative. Work with your teacher and other class members so that every student does something different. Plan a search strategy to find at least 2 print sources and 2 Internet sources to get information on the technology.

Day 2 Students will use the library or resource centre to conduct research, making bibliographic notes immediately so they do not forget their sources. For Internet sites, students should be advised to get the URL as well as the producer of the information.

Day 3 Students will continue to use the library or resource centre to conduct research as above.

Day 4 Students will make a rough copy and have a friend read over the rough copy, checking for spelling mistakes, typographical errors, and thoughts that do not flow smoothly. Students will consult with the teacher to determine what can done to make it better.

Day 5 Students will hand in their report, ensuring to include a title page with student's name, the teacher's name, the class and date.

Equipment, Preparation and Resources (class of 24)

Be sure to reserve the library or resource centre for at least two of the five days. Have some examples of print resources on hand in the science class room.

Categories: | **Assessment and Evaluation**
Knowledge: | Content presented is relevant and coherent
Inquiry: | Library and Internet research skills evident in content
Communication: | Clarity and completeness of the writing.
Applications, Extensions: | Appreciation of economic, environmental, and social issues

Exploring Ecosystems

10 Applied Science Teacher Guide

Project 4.2: The Case for Vegetarians

Learning Expectations 3.02; 3.06: Describe ways in which the relationships between living organisms and their ecosystems are viewed by other cultures; explain changes in popular views about the sustainability of ecosystems and human's responsibility in preserving them.

Connections: Sciencepower 10 : pp. 6 - 7
                  Science 10 : pp. 38, 106
Science 10 Concepts and Connections: NA

Pedagogical Issues

At present, Earth can produce sufficient food to feed all human inhabitants. Yet, at least 20 million people are so undernourished (their food has insufficient energy content) or malnourished (their food has insufficient nutrient content) that they suffer ill health. The focus of this activity is to look at food with reference to energy, energy loss between trophic levels and the decisions we make with reference to the food crops and livestock raised for human consumption. Students need to know that their choices have an impact on global food resources and the energy available for the entire human population.

Science Issues

Many of us, particularly within the western culture, consume food derived primarily from animal sources. These animals convert plant material into animal material, but approximately 90 % of the energy present in the plant material is lost, primarily to heat. This energy conversion has consequences for the planet, particularly with reference to land use and carrying capacity.

In less developed nations, animals consume plant materials that are unsuitable for human consumption. That is, they graze on marginal or sub-marginal agricultural land, converting low quality plant material into animal protein that is useful food. However, in the west, and more developed nations, food animals consume grains and other high quality food that is suitable for human consumption. In other words, these livestock are made to compete with humans for food. Additionally, raising plants for food for animals for food for humans results in an approximate 90 % loss in the amount of energy that could be available to support a growing human population.

The energy required to produce food energy can be expressed as a ratio: a lower number is an indication of reduced environmental impact.

Energy input / Food energy	Food Source
10	Feedlot beef
3.0	Grass-fed beef
3.0	Intensive egg production
2.2	Grass-fed milk
1.9	Coastal fishing
0.9	Range-fed beef
0.9	Intensive corn
0.6	Intensive soybeans
0.3	Low intensity wheat
1.	Low intensity rice

Research Project

Science and Pedagogy

Some starting points for Internet research:

http://www.veg.ca/noframes/index.html
This site provides Toronto-area people with information on maintaining a healthy, ethical, and ecological lifestyle.

http://www.vegetariantimes.com/
Information on vegetarian lifestyles.

http://www.colba.net/~ajstrong/resources.htm
Vegetarian cooking and food issues.

The Learning Activity

Most of the energy present in plants is lost in their conversion to meat. By consuming plants directly, this loss of energy is avoided. Should we all be vegetarians? Over a period of five days, students will prepare to debate this issue as part of a 4-person team. Students will be called upon to present either side, so it is important that they prepare an argument for both sides, working as a team with a coordinated approach.

Day 1   Students will begin to prepare a case for becoming vegetarian, building their case by using facts and adding emotion, and practicing their style on each other.

Day 2   Students will prepare a case for eating meat. Since this is the current practice, they will look for reasons why we eat meat. Students should use a nutritional approach, and focus on the tradition of meat in the diet of many races and cultures.

Day 3   Students will continue to prepare for the debate by practicing to debate. If available, students should find a quiet area and practice how they will debate by facing off 2 against 2.

Day 4   Students will debate.

Day 5   As a class you will review and dissect the key arguments presented by both sides.

Equipment, Preparation and Resources (class of 24)
Reserve the library, resource center, or other quiet area for use by students to prepare for the debate.

Categories: **Assessment and Evaluation**
Knowledge: Facts presented are scientifically accurate
Inquiry: Depth of investigation evident in comments
Communication: Clear, concise, coherent marshaling of arguments
Applications, Extensions: Recognizes personal choices collectively have global impact

Ross Lattner Educational Consultants

Exploring Ecosystems

Chapter 2: Student Exercises

Knowledge and Understanding

Two laws and one theory are emphasized in this unit. The 1st Law of Thermodynamics states that *energy is neither created or destroyed, but is converted from one form to another.* The 2nd Law states that *each time energy is converted into another form, some of that energy is degraded into a lower quality form.* In addition, you will learn new ideas about how matter is cycled among the components of ecosystems. Additional concepts will be introduced as needed.

We will work with diagrams and models to illustrate how human activity influences ecosystems. Knowledge and understanding will be demonstrated at regular intervals through the exercises, so that you can do your best when they are assigned.

Inquiry and Thinking

As often as possible, we will use the PEOE cycle for most labs and activities. You are expected to frame a question, provide your best prediction, and explain your thinking, using both sentences and diagrams. In other exercises, you will simulate the changes in predator and prey populations and follow the movement of energy and matter through food chains and food webs.

At the end of the unit, you will be given a five day independent project. The project will demonstrate your ability to conduct your own investigation.

Communication

The quality of your arguments is the most important aspect of communication in this chapter. Your arguments consist of sentences, organized into paragraphs, and supported by diagrams or other representations.

Each sentence should be clear and to the point. You will find it best to limit your sentences to two concepts linked together to make a reasonable claim. If you need to relate more than two concepts, add a new sentence.

Applications, Connections and Extensions

Every exercise in this book is designed to support you as you learn appropriate theories and apply them to problems. In the labs, you demonstrate your understanding of a theory only by applying the theory. In the quizzes and projects, you are invited to make further connections and extensions of your learning.

Introduction

10 Applied Science Lab Manual

Introduction: Biology, Ecosystems and Human Activity

In this unit we will look at ecosystems and consider the effect of humans on living and non-living components of ecosystems. The labs and activities in this manual will help to focus your attention on basic concepts in ecology. Throughout this unit you should be asking questions about how you affect the natural processes of the ecosystem in which you live. Additionally, you should be curious about how the actions of other people, businesses, and government agencies affect the sustainability of life.

This unit consists of 3 main ideas:

1. Thermodynamic Principles

The universe is made up of just two things: matter and energy. As we learned in Grade 9, matter is what makes up organisms, the food and nutrients that they consume, and the wastes that they produce. Energy is defined as the ability to do work. Energy transformations between **Producers** and **Consumers** play an important role in the functioning of ecosystems.

Organisms use energy to move, perform metabolic functions, and to produce more organisms. All of these energy transformations occur in accordance with **The 1st Law of Thermodynamics**: *Energy is neither created or destroyed, but is converted from one form to another.*

Unfortunately for us, energy transformations are never 100% efficient - there is always loss - usually some energy ends up as heat. Heat energy is less ordered, that is, more random than other higher quality forms of energy. Heat is lower quality energy because it is less able to do useful work. The principle which underlies the loss of heat during energy transformations is referred to as **The 2nd Law of Thermodynamics**, which states: *each time energy is converted into another form, some of that energy is degraded into a lower quality form.*

2. Energy Transfer and Matter Cycling in Ecosystems

All organic molecules that make up the tissues of living organisms are highly ordered and contain high potential energy. Living organisms obtain their energy either by consuming or by producing high energy organic molecules. Producers, plants and their aquatic counterparts Cyanobacteria and Algae, are able to produce high energy molecules from carbon dioxide and light energy from the sun. Consumers eat plants or other consumers that ate plants to obtain matter and energy.

The movement of matter and energy among components of ecosystems accounts for the variety of relationships and organisms that exist. When matter is cycled in ecosystems, there is no loss, in accordance with the **Law of Conservation of Mass**, which was part of the Grade 9 curriculum. However, as we learned above, in any energy transfer there is always a loss of energy. In fact, most energy, approximately 90%, is lost in the transfer between feeding or trophic levels. This energy loss will have profound effects on food chains and webs.

Introduction

3. Abiotic and Biotic Parameters in Ecosystems

A community of living organisms, together with the nonliving factors with which it interacts, is called an ecosystem. An ecosystem regulates the transfer of energy, ultimately derived from the sun, and the cycling of essential elements on which the lives of its plants, animals, and other organisms depend. The nonliving or abiotic parameters of an aquatic ecosystem that we will investigate include levels of oxygen, pH, phosphates, alkalinity, ammonia, nitrate, chloride, and temperature of the water. We will also look for the presence of several species of fish that can indicate the ecological condition of an ecosystem.

All of these ideas are needed to adequately explain how humans affect ecosystems. You will be required to both memorize the main points, and to apply them to problems in this book.

In all of the exercises in this book, the question must be answered in *complete sentences*. One sentence is one thought. A single word is simply not enough.

10 Applied Science Lab Manual

Exploring Ecosystems

Activity 1.1: Building Perpetual Motion Machines

Do you Remember? If not, look up and define the following terms from your text:

Matter:_____
_____

Energy:_____
_____

Thermodynamics:_____
_____

What's The Question?
The laws of thermodynamics states that energy is neither created nor destroyed, but may be converted from one form into another, and that *each time energy is converted into another form, some of that energy is degraded into a lower quality form.* Is it possible to build a perpetual motion machine?

What Are We Doing?
1. Using your wind-up toy, or one provided by your teacher, **predict** how long the apparatus will run.
2. **Explain** why you made your prediction. Do not just guess. Make a reasonable statement based on experience.
3. **Observe** how long the toy ran. Make some changes to see if you can get the toy to run longer. For example, how long does it run with one complete revolution of winding? How many times can you wind the devise? Make several attempts.
4. **Explain** how you were able to affect the length of time the toy operated. What appears to be operating to slow or stop the operation of the toy? Can you overcome these forces?

What Are We Thinking About?
1. Look for places or operations performed by the toy where energy is degraded, such as actions that cause heat or friction. Remember, sound is also a form of radiant energy produced by some mechanical motion.
2. What can you do to minimize the losses of energy to heat or friction?
3. Do you think it is possible to make your wind-up toy operate for an indefinite period of time. If so, how is this possible? If not, what force appears to most important in causing the device to stop operation?

Questions For Later...(to be answered in your notebook)
1. Why is it not possible to build a machine that will operate indefinitely with no input of energy?

2. What is the immediate source of energy for your wind-up toy?

3. What is the source of your energy that allows you to wind up the wind-up toy? What is the source of all energy on planet earth? What happens to most of this energy?

Thermodynamic Principles

Name:
Date:

Focus Question: Write the question that you are trying to answer.

1 **Predict**: Will the wind-up toy (*perpetual motion machine*) continue to operate for an indefinite period of time?

2 **Explain** your prediction. Use your understanding and experience with mechanical things and wind-up toys and write a paragraph.

3 **Observe** and record your observations. Make a table to show how long the toy operates for a certain amount of energy input (*i.e.*, number of rotations of winding).

4 **Explain** your observations. Use the 1st and 2nd laws of thermodynamics and write a complete paragraph.

Activity 1.2: Photosynthesis and Respiration

Do you Remember? If not, look up and define the following terms from your text:

nutrient:_____

_____

photosynthesis:_____

_____

respiration:_____

_____

What's The Question?
Photosynthesis and respiration are essentially the same chemical reaction operating in different directions. The purpose of this activity is to observe how these two events operate to cycle matter, such as carbon and water, and energy from one form into another.

What Are We Doing?
1. Use a straw and exhale into the solution as directed by your teacher. Next, your teacher will collect gas released from a living aquatic plant. **Predict** the type of gas produced by you and the aquatic plant.
2. **Explain** how you knew what type of gas was produced and what factors might affect the amount of gas produced by you and the plant.
3. **Observe** the chemical tests used to determine the types of gases produced by animals and plants. Record your observations.
4. Use word equations to **Explain** the processes of respiration and photosynthesis. Are these processes simply reverse chemical reactions? What is the role of energy, and where does the energy come from in each process?

What Are We Thinking About?
1. Look for similarities in the reactants and products of the two chemical processes.
2. What substances are common to both photosynthesis and respiration?
3. How is energy involved in each chemical process?
4. When do plants carry out photosynthesis? Do plants respire?
5. When do your cells respire?
6. What happens to the CO_2 that you exhale?
7. What happens to the oxygen produced by plants?

Questions For Later...(to be answered in your notebook)
1. What are **fossil fuels**, how were they formed, and what gases are produced when these fuels are burned?

2. The source of energy for photosynthesis is solar radiation. Use your textbook or the Internet to obtain an estimate of the percentage of solar radiation actually used by plants for photosynthesis on a global basis.

3. What happens to all of the sun's energy striking the earth that is not used for photosynthesis?

Thermodynamic Principles

Name:
Date:

Focus Question: Write the question that you are trying to answer.

1 *Predict:* What gases do you exhale? What gas is produced by a photosynthesizing plant?

2 *Explain* what led you to your prediction. Use your current understanding of respiration and photosynthesis.

3 *Observe* and record your observations of the chemical tests. Describe the chemical tests for oxygen and carbon dioxide. What factors might affect the rate of production of these gases?

4 *Explain* the processes of respiration and photosynthesis using word equations. How are the products of one reaction related to the reactants of the other? How is energy involved in these chemical reactions?

Exploring Ecosystems

10 Applied Science Lab Manual

Activity 2.1: Where Does Your Recyclable Material Go?

Reduce, Reuse, Recycle. These are the three R's of waste management. When we recycle our discarded materials we are mimicking the natural processes occurring in ecosystems.

In many communities in southern Ontario, recyclable materials are placed in or beside a plastic **blue box** for collection. Some of the items that can be recycled include the following: clean plastic bags, newspapers and magazines, box board and mixed paper, empty metal aerosol and paint cans, plastic bottles and jugs, rigid and foam plastic containers, aluminum trays and foil, glass bottles and jars, and metal food and beverage cans.

What's The Question?
Recycling can reduce the negative effect humans have on the planet, but only if we ensure that recycled materials reduce our need to consume more natural resources. In this activity, we consider what becomes of the items that go into our blue boxes and how this reduces overall consumption.

What Are We Doing?
1. Record or estimate the number of items in each category listed above that your family used during the last 7 days, multiply these numbers by the number of students in your class, and **Predict** the amount of material that your class could have recycled this week.
2. **Explain** how this prediction, or estimate is imperfect, but a reasonable first step in determining the amount of material recycled.
3. Data on the two pages provides an estimate of the value of each category of recycled goods, the cost of recycling programs, where the recycled items are used, and the amount of natural resources conserved by the recycling process. Use these data to calculate how much your family and class have reduced consumption of natural resources.

What Are We Thinking About?
1. How much does it cost to recycle? How much money is generated by municipal recycling programs?
2. Are any of the recycled items simply reused? Why are most items changed in some way prior to subsequent use?
3. How much glass, aluminum, and steel is recovered in recycling programs? How many of each item are required for a mass of 1 kg? Does recycling result in less need for costly and potentially environmentally harmful mining operations?
4. Why is saving energy important from both a local and global perspective?

Questions For Later...(to be answered in your notebook)
1. Explain the changes that plastics go through when they are recycled. How is this an example of the Laws of Thermodynamics?

2. Find out if your school has a recycling program. If so, find out what problems were encountered by the group or individual responsible. If not, find out what reasons prevent your school from enacting a recycling program.

3. Explain why saving energy actually results in savings of natural resources.

Cycling Matter in Ecosystems

Name:
Date:

Focus Question: Write the question that you are trying to answer.

1 *Predict*: the number of items of each of the following used by your family and class during the last seven days.

Item	Family	Class
Plastic bags		
Newspapers		
Magazines		
Paint cans		
Rigid foam plastic containers		
Aluminum trays		
Glass bottles and jars		
Soft drink cans		
Food cans		

2 *Explain* the assumptions that you used to make your prediction.

3 *Observe*: Use this space to calculate the potential amount of money, material, and energy saved by your family and class through recycling.

Amount Conserved

Item	Mass (kg)	Money	Energy (kWh)

4 *Explain* the value of recycling with reference to money, matter, and energy.

10 Applied Science Information Sheet

Exploring Ecosystems

The Monetary Value of Recyclable Material

The following data are based on information obtained in July, 1998, from **Centre and South Hastings Waste Service**. This recycling program has been operating in Trenton and surrounding Hastings and Prince Edward Counties since 1990. While these data many not apply specifically to your location, they are useful for comparison purposes. All dollar values are expressed in Canadian Dollars.

Cost of recycling: $95 /1000 kg **Cost of disposal in landfill site:** $150 /1000 kg

Recycled Material	Value $/1000kg	Subsequent Use
Clear glass	49.00	Crushed and mixed with sand, limestone, and soda ash (same things that new glass is made from), heated to 1550^0 C, molded into new bottles and jars
Colored glass	24.25	Reprocessed into fibreglass, glass beads, reflective paint, or used as aggregate in asphalt and sewer pipe
Aluminum cans and foil	1,403.60	Shredded, paint removed, melted down into ingots, rolled into sheets, reformed into new cans
Steel (tin) cans	85.90	Steel separated from tin then both are melted down into ingots, rolled into sheets, reformed into new cans
Polyethylene terephthalate (PET - plastic Code 1)	379.94	Ground, pelletized, and extruded to form soft drink bottles, car bumpers, and fibre fill
High density polyethylene (HDPE - plastic Code 2)	347.60	Ground, pelletized, and extruded to form bleach jugs, blue boxes, toys, laundry baskets
Polyvinyl chloride (PVC - plastic Code 3)	85.90	Ground, pelletized, and extruded to form mouthwash bottles, plastic drain pipe
Low density polyethylene (LDPE - plastic Code 4)	44.00	Ground, pelletized, and extruded to form margarine container lids, pallets, plastic lumber
Polypropylene (PP - plastic Code 5)	44.00	Ground, pelletized, and extruded to form margarine containers, twine, rope
Polystyrene (PS - plastic Code 6)	20.00	Ground, pelletized, and extruded to form coffee cups, packaging, trays, video and audio cassettes, rigid foam insulation
Newspapers & magazines	40.00	Paper is de-inked, reprocessed into newsprint, tissue, paper towels, napkins
White paper	125.00	Added to recycled paper to improve quality
Box board	30	Re-pulped, processed into laundry detergent boxes

Cycling Matter in Ecosystems

10 Applied Science Information Sheet

Natural Resources Conserved by Recycling Material

The following information was obtained from **Centre and South Hastings Waste Service** and reflect data for the total amount of materials recycled between September, 1990 and June, 1998. While these data may not apply specifically to your location, they are useful for comparison purposes.

Recycled Material	Amount Recycled (kg)	Energy Conserved (kWh)	Natural Resources Conserved
paper	60 744 000	249 475 000	1 137 600 trees & 82 570 000 kg of CO_2
glass	13 850	13 433 000	primarily energy
plastic	5900	164 527 000	47 605 000 L of crude oil
steel	7570	54 518 000	primarily energy
aluminum	1775	26 425 000	primarily energy

Exploring Ecosystems

10 Applied Science Lab Manual

Activity 2.2: A Great Lakes Food Web

Do you Remember? Look up and define the following terms:

producer:_____

_____

consumer:_____

_____

trophic level:_____

_____

What's The Question?
Photosynthesis and respiration are essentially the same chemical reaction operating in different directions. The purpose of this activity is to observe how these two events operate to cycle matter, such as carbon and water, and energy from one form into another.

What Are We Doing?
1. Organize the organisms found in **Food Chains 1 - 4** of the **Information Page** into a food chain (*i.e.,* top carnivore on top with producers on the bottom).
2. Assume that the biomass of producers in each food chain is 1 000 000 kg and that only 10 % of the biomass is retained between trophic levels. Calculate the amount of biomass present at each level in the food chains.
3. Draw a biomass pyramid in the space provided, using a 1 cm x 1 cm square for each 1000 kg of biomass.
4. Draw links between the food chains using arrows from predator to prey or consumer to producer. Neatly, transfer your completed food web to the space provided.

What Are We Thinking About?
1. What is the source of all Earth's energy?
2. By what process are producers able to convert solar energy into food energy?
3. What causes energy to be lost at each step up a food chain?
4. Generally speaking, will there be more individuals at the top or bottom of a food chain?
5. Is it possible for a consumer to eat more than one type of producer?
6. Is it possible for a carnivore to eat more than one type of prey?

Questions For Later...(to be answered in your notebook)
1. Explain what happens to the amount of energy present in a lower trophic level and the energy present in the next higher trophic level.

2. What would happen to animals in higher trophic levels if most of the producers became contaminated with a chemical like mercury? Explain what would happen to the level of mercury in the living tissues of animals in higher trophic levels.

3. If more top carnivores, say lake trout, were added to the Great Lake in an artificial stocking program, could the ecosystem support these added carnivores indefinitely?

Cycling Matter in Ecosystems

Name:
Date:

Focus Question: Write the question that you are trying to answer.

Food Chains 1 and 2	Food Chains 3 and 4
Biomass Pyramid	**Great Lakes Food Web** ß

10 Applied Science Information Sheet

Exploring Ecosystems

A GREAT LAKES FOOD WEB

The following data are biological information about common species found in the Great Lakes. Use these data to organize food chains and eventually a food web.

Food Chain 1
mosquito larva
algae
freshwater shrimp
slimy sculpin
rainbow trout

Food Chain 2
phytoplankton
mayfly nymph
yellow perch
walleye
osprey

Food Chain 3
lake trout
lake herring
blackfly larvae
Canada water weed

Food Chain 4
duck weed
mallard duckling
snapping turtle
rainbow smelt
muskellunge

Biological Information For Selected Great Lakes Species

Species	Ecology
mosquito larva	• feed on algae • prey for larger animals
algae	• microscopic plants
freshwater shrimp	• prey for larger animals • omnivorous predators
sunfish	• omnivorous predator • prey for larger animals
rainbow trout	• omnivorous predator • prey for larger animals
phytoplankton	• produce food by photosynthesis
mayfly nymphs	• feed on microscopic plant organisms • prey for larger animals
yellow perch	• omnivorous predator • prey for larger animals
walleye	• omnivorous predator • prey for larger animals
water weed	• aquatic plant
osprey	• predator of fish

Species	Ecology
lake trout	• omnivorous predator
lake herring	• consume plankton, nymphs, and other aquatic insects • prey for yellow perch and walleye
blackfly larvae	• filter feed small bits of organic material • prey for larger animals
duck weed	• small floating aquatic plant
mallard duckling	• eats small aquatic plants and aquatic insects • prey for muskellunge and snapping turtle
snapping turtle	• omnivorous predator
rainbow smelt	• feed on plankton, aquatic insects and small fish • prey for lake trout and walleye
muskellunge	• omnivorous predator

Ross Lattner Educational Consultants   www.rosslattner.ca

10 Applied Science Lab Manual

Exploring Ecosystems

Activity 2.3: Predators and Prey - A Simulation

Do you Remember? Look up and define the following terms

predator:_____
_____

prey:_____
_____

population:_____
_____

What's The Question?
In many species, the number of individuals fluctuates for reasons which are not readily apparent. However, it can be shown that a relationship exists between the numbers of predators and prey in many ecosystems. In this activity, we will investigate a simulated predator-prey relationship.

What Are We Doing?

1. If the number of individuals of a prey population increase, **Predict** what will happen to the number of predators.

2. **Explain** whether this will happen right away, or will there be some delay.

3. Use the population data provided by your teacher to prepare a graph of the numbers of lynx and snowshoe hare. Use one colour for hare and another for lynx. **Observe** the amount of time between peaks in their numbers.

4. **Explain** what might cause the numbers of hare to increase and then fall and the delay between peaks in the numbers of hare and peaks in the numbers of lynx.

What Are We Thinking About?

1. Snow shoe hare feed on vegetation. In winter they browse on twigs, buds, and bark (especially the cambium layer). During summer they consume a wide variety of succulent vegetation.

2. Hare give birth to 2-3 litters of 2 - 4 young (called leverets) from April to August.

3. Lynx feed almost exclusively on snow shoe hare, but will supplement their diet with rodents and birds.

4. Lynx give birth usually to two young which are born during March and April.

Questions For Later...(to be answered in your notebook)

1. What factors would limit the number of snow shoe hare? What factors limit the number of lynx?

2. If there were no lynx present, do you think hare numbers would continue to fluctuate? Explain.

3. What effect could the introduction of another predator have on the hare population?

4. Usually, there are more individuals in prey populations in comparison to predators? Why is this so?

Cycling Matter in Ecosystems

Name:
Date:

Focus Question: Write the question that you are trying to answer.

1 If the number of individuals of a prey population increase, **Predict** what will happen to the number of predators.

2 **Explain** whether this will happen right away, or will there be some delay.

3 On a separate sheet of graph paper, plot the numbers of hare and lynx during the 50 years for which the data cover. **Observe** the relationship between peaks in the numbers of lynx and hare. Calculate this time lag and write it here.

4 **Explain** what might cause the numbers of hare to increase and then fall and the delay between peaks in the numbers of hare and peaks in the numbers of lynx.

Ross Lattner Educational Consultants   47   www.rosslattner.ca

10 Applied Science Lab Manual

Exploring Ecosystems

Activity 2.4: Components of an Ecosystem

Do you Remember? List 4 compounds or elements that are cycled through ecosystems.
1. _____
2. _____
3. _____
4. _____

What's The Question?
An ecosystem is a group of living organisms that form a self-regulating system with their non-living environment through which energy and materials transfer. We will attempt to set up such a self-sustaining system, then return to it after some time. Our purpose is to determine what components are necessary to ensure that energy and materials are adequately transferred to sustain life.

What Are We Doing?
1. You will need a large glass jar with a screw-top lid, clean sand or fine gravel, clean water, aquatic plants, at least one snail, and at least one small herbivorous or omnivorous fish. **Predict** how long you will be able to keep your fish alive without removing the lid, or changing the model ecosystem in any way. Follow your teacher's instructions to set up your model ecosystem, then proceed to step 2.
2. **Explain** what role is played by each of the components of your model ecosystem in cycling matter and sustaining conditions for life.
3. **Observe** the activities of your ecosystem over the course of your investigation. Note any changes in appearance and when they occurred.
4. At the end of your investigation, **Explain** the changes that occurred with reference to interruptions in cycling of matter and energy.

What Are We Thinking About?
1. Why must the model ecosystem be placed near a bright window?

2. Why did you wait at least one day after filling the jar with sand and water before adding the plants, snails, and fish?

3. What do plants do?

4. What do the snails and fish eat?

5. How do these plants and animals obtain their oxygen?

6. What happens to the carbon dioxide produced by the fish and snails?

7. What happens to other waste products?

Questions For Later...(to be answered in your notebook)
1. If the model ecosystem was placed on a sensitive electronic balance, do you think it would change in mass? Explain your answer completely.

2. What do you think would happen to the model ecosystem if the snails were removed? Identify the ecological role filled by the snail.

3. What is the ecological role of the sand or gravel?

Cycling Matter in Ecosystems

Name:
Date:

Focus Question: Write the question that you are trying to answer.

1 *Predict* how long you will be able to keep your fish alive without removing the lid, or changing the model ecosystem in any way.

2 *Explain* what role is played by each of the components of your model ecosystem in cycling matter and sustaining conditions for life.

3 *Observe* the activities of your ecosystem over the course of your investigation. Note any changes in appearance and when they occurred.

4 *Explain* the changes that occurred with reference to interruptions in cycling of matter and energy.

10 Applied Science
Lab Manual

Exploring Ecosystems

Activity 2.5: Competition

New words: Look up the following terms:
1. Mutualism:_____
   _____
2. Comensalism:_____
   _____
3. Symbiosis: _____
   _____

What's The Question?
Since all resources are limited to some degree, individuals must **compete** for these resources. Competition can exist not only between species in a given area, but also among individuals within the same species in a given area. The former is called *inter*specific, whereas the latter form of competition is called *intra*specific. Today, we investigate both types of competition.

What Are We Doing?
1. You will need 5 small containers (*e.g.,* coffee cups), potting soil, 12 spinach seeds, and 12 corn seeds. Make tiny holes in the bottom of the coffee cups to allow excess water to escape. Fill the cups to the same depth with potting soil. In container **A**, plant 3 corn seeds. In **B**, plant 3 spinach seeds. In **C**, plant 6 corn seeds. In **D**, plant 6 spinach seeds. In **E**, plant 3 corn and 3 spinach seeds. Be sure to plant all seeds equally to a depth of 1.5 cm. Add the same amount of water to each container - just enough to make the soil moist, not flooded. **Predict** which container will support the greatest growth.
2. **Explain** your prediction with reference to the competition for resources by individuals within and between species. Maintain your plants as instructed by your teacher.
3. After about 3 weeks, **Observe** the appearance of each container and determine the average mass of a corn and a spinach plant in each container with an electronic balance. Share your data.
4. **Explain** your results.

What Are We Thinking About?
1. Why do we plant all seeds to approximately the same depth?

2. Why do we plant corn with corn and spinach with spinach?

3. Why do we plant corn and spinach in the same container?

4. Why do we use three plants to determine the average mass of one plant?

5. What kind of nutrients do spinach and corn require to grow well?

Questions For Later...(to be answered in your notebook)
1. Which type of competition, inter- or intra- specific, appears to produce the smallest average mass, and therefore, is more intense.

2. Some gardeners inter-plant different species (*e.g.,* bean and corn plants) in the same row. Why might this be a good use of resources and space?

Cycling Matter in Ecosystems

Name:
Date:

Focus Question: Write the question that you are trying to answer.

1 *Predict* which container will support the greatest growth.

2 *Explain* your prediction with reference to the competition for resources by individuals within and between species.

3 *Observe* the appearance of each container and determine the average mass of a corn and a spinach plant in each container with an electronic balance.

4 *Explain* what your findings suggest about inter- and intraspecific competition.

Exploring Ecosystems

10 Applied Science Lab Manual

Activity 2.6: Your School Yard - An Ecosystem Out of Balance

Do you Remember? Explain the following terms:

water cycle: _____

_____

nitrogen cycle: _____

_____

carbon cycle: _____

_____

What's The Question?
Ecosystems function by cycling matter and energy between living and non-living components. Is this happening in your school yard? We will consider what happens to the plant and animal species growing there and the energy and nutrients which can be found there.

What Are We Doing?
1. On the next page, draw diagrams of the carbon, nitrogen, and water cycles that involve your school yard. In each cycle, look for incomplete loops. For example, perhaps your school yard is watered during hot weather. Most of this water evaporates, a small portion is transpired by plants, and almost no water infiltrates the soil to become groundwater. **Explain** how each of these cycles is somehow affected.

2. In your notebook, draw food chains for the consumers and producers living in your school yard. Link these food chains together into a food web and draw this in the space provided on the next page. Again, look for actions that disturb the cycling of nutrients through this ecosystem.

What Are We Thinking About?
1. What happens to the solar radiation striking the ground? What happens to the grass, weeds, and other vegetation? For example, perhaps you school cuts the grass and then disposes of these grass clippings in the local landfill site. Do you have any trees? Do these trees drop their leaves in autumn, and if so, what happens to them?

2. Are fertilizers applied to the school yard? If so, what are they? Are pesticides or herbicides applied to the school yard?

3. What kind of insects grow on the school yard? What kind of birds can be seen feeding on the yard? Would mammals also be found on the school yard?

Questions For Later...(to be answered in your notebook)

1. Some pesticides applied to lawns and gardens are not specific in terms of the insects killed. What negative effects could result from applying these pesticides?

2. Fertilizers applied to improve plant growth on lands can find their way into streams and lakes. What negative effects could be expected?

3. Do you think your school yard is an ecosystem out of balance? Explain your answer completely.

Cycling Matter in Ecosystems

Name:
Date:

Focus Question: Write the question that you are trying to answer.

1 *Water Cycle*

2 *Carbon Cycle*

3 *Nitrogen Cycle*

4 *Food Web*

10 Applied Science
Lab Manual

Exploring Ecosystems

Lab 3.1: Happiness is a Healthy Local Waterway

Do you Remember? **List 4 abiotic factors that influence water quality.**
1. _____
2. _____
3. _____
4. _____

What's The Question?
Organisms generally live where conditions are suitable for their requirements. Chemical factors in water are very important in determining where fish are found and in what numbers. In this investigation we will use water chemistry tests to analyze the quality of water in a pond, stream, or lake to predict whether or not various species of fish can survive in the water.

What Are We Doing?
1. Prior to your field trip, **Predict** the species of fish you expect to find in the waterway.

2. **Explain** why you believe the conditions of this waterway are suitable for these species to survive.

3. During your field trip, **Observe** the features of the waterway as instructed by your teacher. In addition, you will perform up to 8 chemical tests on the water. Record data on the next page.

4. **Explain**, using your observations and the data you collected, why this waterway is able to support the species it does. The data available from the **Information Page** will help you to make your decision.

What Are We Thinking About?
1. How does oxygen get into the water that you sampled? What abiotic and biotic factor appears to have the greatest effect on the amount of dissolved oxygen? How do high phosphate and nitrate levels tend to lower the level of dissolved oxygen in waterways?

2. What factors contribute to the level of acidity and alkalinity in water?

3. How does ammonia enter into waterways?

4. What could account for a high level of chloride in the water?

5. What type of substrate (*i.e.*, gravel, sand or mud) exists on the bottom of the waterway?

Questions For Later...(to be answered in your notebook)
1. If untreated water was allowed to run off of city streets directly into a waterway, what effects could you predict on the chemical factors that your class measured?

2. Why is it sometimes possible to find carp living in waterways that appear to be incompatible for fish like trout? Explain your answer with reference to some of the chemical factors that you sampled?

3. How does water temperature affect the level of dissolved oxygen in waterways?

Abiotic and Biotic Factors

Name:
Date:

Focus Question: Write the question that you are trying to answer.

1 *Predict* the species of fish you expect to find in the waterway.

2 *Explain* why you believe the conditions of this waterway are suitable for these species to survive.

3 *Observe* the features and record data from the waterway as instructed by your teacher.

4 *Explain* using your observations and the data you collected, why this waterway is able to support the species it does.

Chemical Tests	Station 1	Station 2	Station 3
Oxygen			
pH			
Phosphates			
Alkalinity			
Ammonia			
Nitrate			
Chloride			
Temperature			

Cycling Matter in Ecosystems

10 Applied Science Information Sheet

Abiotic Factors Affecting Aquatic Ecosystems

Chemical factors can determine what types of fish survive in certain waterways. The following information will assist you in predicting what species of fish might survive in the waterway that you sample. Use this information to justify your prediction.

Dissolved Oxygen

Many gasses are able to dissolve in water. Usually, more gas dissolves as the temperature of the water decreases. Oxygen is most soluble in water near 0 °C. Oxygen dissolves in water primarily from air mixed into water by turbulence in a process known as aeration. Aquatic organisms remove oxygen from solution during respiration. This is especially evident when bacteria decompose organic matter present in waterways and significantly deplete the amount of dissolved oxygen.

pH is a measurement of the amount of hydrogen ions in solution, ranging from 0 (extremely acidic) to 14 (extremely basic). A pH of 7 is neutral. Most fish species can tolerate a pH of between 6 and 8. At less than pH 5 or greater than pH 9, fish cannot adequately obtain oxygen or remove carbon dioxide across their gill membranes. Acid precipitation, especially in areas where the underlying bedrock does not contain limestone (which tends to neutralize acids), can contribute to acidic pH in water.

Chlorides

Salt (sodium chloride) is the source of most chloride in water. Although a small amount of chloride is naturally present, most salt enters waterways from road salt applied to improve winter driving conditions. Fish habitat quality is impaired when chloride levels exceed 50 mg/L.

Alkalinity

Water with dissolved carbonates and other minerals from limestone bedrock is said to be alkaline. Alkalinity is necessary to neutralize acids. Alkalinity also results from living things that produce carbon dioxide during respiration. Hence, a high alkalinity measurement in water is evidence of a productive ecosystem. In limestone areas, alkalinity should range between 100 and 250 mg/L. In waters over granitic bedrock, the level of alkalinity will not usually exceed 50 mg/L.

Phosphates are important nutrients that are naturally present in low levels in water systems. However, phosphates from our home, industrial, and agricultural products (*e.g.,* fertilizers, detergents, etc.) can enter water systems, leading to an overabundance of algae, and subsequent depletion of dissolved oxygen. Phosphate levels in excess of 0.015 mg/L are generally considered unsuitable for fish.

Ammonia and Nitrates contain nitrogen, which is part of proteins, and therefore present in all living things. Nitrogen exists in water as part of ammonia or nitrates. Ammonia enters waterways through decay of human or animal sewage and from agricultural runoff. Nitrates enter waterways by the same processes. The quality of fish habitat is impaired when ammonia levels exceed 0.5 mg/L or nitrate levels exceed 0.3 mg/L.

Data adapted from Andrews and McEwan. 1987. *Investigating Aquatic Ecosystems.* Prentice-Hall Canada Inc.

Exploring Ecosystems

Habitat Features for Seven Species of Ontario Fish

Fish	Temperature Range (0°C)	Optimum Temperature (0°C)	Minimum Dissolved Oxygen (mg/L)	pH Range
Rainbow trout	5 - 20	15	4.6	5.5 - 8.2
Walleye	0 - 30	21	3.0	5.5 - 8.2
Smallmouth bass	2 - 32	28	4.0	5.5 - 8.2
Yellow perch	4 - 32	20	5.0	4.8 - 8.2
Crappie	2 - 35	28	2.5	5.0 - 9.0
Catfish	4 - 35	30	2.5	5.0 - 9.0
Carp	4 - 35	32	1.0	5.0 - 9.0

Source: Andrews and McEwan. 1987. *Investigating Aquatic Ecosystems.* Prentice-Hall Canada Inc. & Scott and Crossman. 1973. *Freshwater Fishes of Canada*. Bulletin 184, Fisheries Research Board of Canada, Ottawa.

Exploring Ecosystems and Humans

10 Applied Science Lab Manual

Lab 3.2: Mercury in Fish and Bioaccumulation

Do you Remember? If not, look up the definition of the following term:
concentration: _____
_____

What's The Question?

Mercury is a silvery-white heavy metal that remains liquid at room temperature. We know of its use in thermometers, but it is also used to prevent growth of fungi and pulp and paper mills. Through accident or neglect, some mercury has found its way into the Great Lakes. Fish take in certain mercury compounds from the water through their gills and in their food, thereby concentrating the amount in their flesh. Larger fish of the same species in the same lake or river usually have a higher level of contamination than smaller fish because they are older and have longer to accumulate mercury in their tissues. Similarly, fish species that are top carnivores have more mercury than fish lower on the food chain. Bioaccumulation is the term used to describe the increasing amounts of substance found in animal tissues as you move higher up the food chain. Since all mercury compounds are toxic when found in sufficient quantity, we would prefer to have no mercury in the fish we consume. However, the federal government has established an acceptable limit for mercury contamination of 0.5 ppm (parts per million). In this activity we will investigate the meaning of ppm and study bioaccumulation using data collected from five species of fish taken from Lake Superior.

What Are We Doing? - Part A

1. You will be given data on concentration of mercury in tissues of four species of fish: lake trout, walleye, pike, and small mouth bass. **Predict** which species of fish will have the highest concentration of mercury.

2. **Explain** your prediction based on size and age of these fish.

3. Using different colours for each species, plot **Concentration of Mercury** on the vertical axis and **Fish Mass** on the horizontal axis. **Observe** the resulting relationship.

4. **Explain** this relationship based on your understanding of bioaccumulation.

What Are We Doing? - Part B

1. Put the contents of one package of grape Koolaid® into a pitcher that you have brought from home, then add 1000 mL of tap water. Pour 100 mL of this full-strength Koolaid® into a beaker and set it aside for later colour comparison. Pour another 100 mL of full-strength Koolaid® into a beaker. Retain the remaining full-strength Koolaid® for later.

2. Dilute 100 mL of full-strength Koolaid® with exactly 900 mL of tap water. Collect 100 mL of diluted Koolaid® for later comparison. Pour another 100 mL of diluted Koolaid® into a beaker. Discard the remainder.

3. Repeat step 2 three more times. When completed you should have 5 beakers for colour comparison.

4. Observe the beakers and calculate the concentration of grape Koolaid® in ppm.

Questions For Later...(to be answered in your notebook)

1. The Guide to Eating Ontario Sport Fish advises consumers that it is safe to eat large salmon but not similarly large lake trout from many parts of Lake Ontario. Why is this so?

2. Investigate bioaccumulation and its effects on peregrine falcon breeding.

Abiotic and Biotic Factors

Name:
Date:

Focus Question: Write the question that you are trying to answer.

1 *Predict* which species of fish will have the highest concentration of mercury.

2 *Explain* your prediction based on size and age of these fish.

3 *Observe* Record your colour observations and show calculations for the concentration in ppm of grape Koolaid®.

4 *Explain* the relationship between size and species of fish and concentration of mercury.

Abiotic and Biotic Factors

10 Applied Science Information Sheet

Concentration of Mercury in Tissues of Four Species of Great Lakes Fish

(data collected in 1978 - 1981, Minnesota Pollution Control Agency)

Species	Mass (kg)	Mercury Concentration (ppm or mg/kg)
Walleye	0.18	0.05
Walleye	0.36	0.10
Walleye	0.77	0.75
Walleye	0.50	0.54
Walleye	1.5	1.10
Northern pike	1.7	0.80
Northern pike	0.68	0.13
Northern pike	1.1	0.47
Northern pike	2.3	1.0
Northern pike	1.1	0.55
Lake trout	0.91	0.21
Lake trout	2.8	1.0
Lake trout	0.77	0.14
Small mouth bass	0.86	0.44
Small mouth bass	0.80	0.30
Small mouth bass	0.45	0.19
Small mouth bass	0.61	0.25

10 Applied Science Lab Manual

Exploring Ecosystems

Lab 3.3: "There's a Desert in Canada?" A Look at Canadian Biomes

What's a Biome? Use your text book and list 6 biomes and their approximate location in Canada.
1. _____
2. _____
3. _____
4. _____
5. _____
6. _____

What's The Question?
Most of Canada is classified as *taiga* - northern boreal forest. Yet, most Canadian cities are found in more southern biomes, such as deciduous forest and grasslands. In this activity we will look at the diversity of Canadian biomes and the plants, animals, and climatic factors that characterize biomes.

What Are We Doing?

1. **Predict** In what biome is your school situated?

2. **Explain** why you believe this is so.

3. **Observe** the accompanying information on biomes of Canada. Place each of the Canadian locations in a biome.

4. **Explain** why you placed each city or location in its particular biome.

What Are We Thinking About?

1. What type of vegetation is most prominent in the area around your school? What type of animals are you most likely to see in the area around your school? Generally, what type of climatic features would you expect for the area around your school?

2. Why do biomes tend to follow bands around the world?

3. Sage brush and other desert species grow in the southern interior of British Columbia, yet the coastal forest can be found less than 100 km west. What factors appear to influence the climate of southern British Columbia?

Questions For Later...(to be answered in your notebook)

1. What do you think would happen to plants transplanted from one biome and then moved to another? Would they continue to survive or would they perish?

2. Wolves were once thought to exist throughout most of Canada, but now they are confined to more northern areas. What factor(s) now limit their range?

3. Prairie chickens were once common throughout Manitoba, Saskatchewan, and Alberta. However, today they are limited to very small parts of south western Manitoba and south eastern Saskatchewan. Why has their range become so much reduced in ?

Abiotic and Biotic Factors

Name:
Date:

Focus Question: Write the question that you are trying to answer.

1 **Predict** In what biome is your school situated?

2 **Explain** why you believe this is so.

3 **Observe** the accompanying information on biomes of Canada. Place each of the Canadian locations in a biome.

4 **Explain** why you placed each city or location in its particular biome.

Exploring Ecosystems

10 Applied Science
Information Sheet

Characteristics of Canadian Biomes

Biome	Indicator Species		Precipitation (equivalent cm)	Temperature	
	Plants	Animals		Winter	Summer
Boreal forest	coniferous trees • pine • spruce • fir	• moose • wolves • spruce grouse	80 - 100	cold	warm
Temperate forest	deciduous trees • maple • beech • oak	• deer • raccoon • opossum • skunk	75 - 100	cool	hot
Coastal rain forest	• western hemlock • western red cedar	• Alaskan brown bear • blue grouse	> 100	mild	cool
Grassland	• grasses • sedges	• swift fox • black footed ferret • prairie chicken	25 - 75	cold	hot
Tundra	• dwarf birch • dwarf willow	• arctic fox • ptarmigan	< 25	frigid	cool
Desert	• prickly pear cactus • sagebrush	• Ord kangaroo rat • sagebrush vole	< 25	cold	hot

Abiotic and Biotic Factors

10 Applied Science Information Sheet

Climate Data for Twelve Canadian Locations

Town/City	Latitude (° N)	Longitude (° W)	Altitude (m)	Jan Mean Daily Min (° C)	July Mean Daily Max (° C)	Mean annual precipitation (cm)
Ecum Secum	45	62	22	-9.4	19.4	142
Swift Current	50	108	816	-17.8	26.1	38
Spring Island	50	127	11	2.8	16.7	279
Ashcroft River	51	121	488	-10.0	28.3	25
Ennadai Lake	62	101	325	-35.0	17.2	23
Ethelda Bay	53	130	0	2.2	17.8	320
Kamloops	51	120	345	-8.3	30.0	25
Cold Lake	54	110	544	-23.9	22.8	51
Chatham	42	82	183	-6.7	28.3	76
Goose Bay	53	60	44	-20.6	21.1	84
Guelph	44	80	334	-10.0	26.1	84
Dryden	50	93	372	-24.4	25.5	69

One step each day, done by Friday...

The Five Day Project

Project 4.1: Energy Technologies

0 Project Instructions

Most of Canada, and indeed the world, relies on energy from fossil fuel sources. What other technologies are currently or potentially available? Each student will prepare a poster presenting important information on at least one energy technology involving a Canadian initiative. The poster should include relevant diagrams along with explanations about the efficiency of the energy transformations at each stage in the generation and transmission of energy.

0 My Plan and Outline

1 Choose an Energy Technology

Work with your teacher and other class members so that every student does something different. Plan a search strategy to find at least 2 print sources and 2 Internet sources to get information on the technology.

1 What technology am I studying? List key words.

Date: / 5

2 Execute Your Search

Use the library or resource centre to conduct research. Make bibliographic notes immediately so that you do not forget your sources. For Internet sites, get the URL as well as the publisher. Look for diagrams that help to explain the technology and the energy conversions involved.

2 Ask your teacher: what is the bibliographic style used in your school? Write your bibliographic information in this space.

Date: / 5

Ross Lattner Educational Consultants   www.rosslattner.ca

One step each day, done by Friday...

The Five Day Project

Project 4.1   Energy Technologies   Name:

3 Use the library or resource centre to conduct research. Make bibliographic notes immediately so that you do not forget your sources. For Internet sites, get the URL as well as the publisher. After today, you should have enough material to make your poster. Plan how you will display your information before you glue things in place. Ask someone for their opinion about the overall appearance of the poster.	**3** How will you present your information? Flow chart? Venn diagram? Computer? Ask your teacher about concept maps and ways to logically organize the facts. Date: / 5
4 Bring your poster-making material to class. Have a friend read over your rough copy, checking for spelling mistakes, typographical errors, and thoughts that do not flow smoothly. Talk to your teacher about your project and what you can do to make it better.	**4** Print the rough copy double-spaced. Make changes with a contrasting colour in the space between lines. Ask other people in the class about your choice of background and foreground colours. Do they understand your approach or the effect that you are trying to achieve. Date: / 5
5 Hand in your poster. Be sure to include your name, the teacher's name, the class and date prominently on the front of the poster.	**5** Date: / 5

Ross Lattner Educational Consultants   67   www.rosslattner.ca

One step each day, done by Friday...

The Five Day Project

Project 4.2: The Case for Vegetarians

0 **Project Instructions**	0 **My Plan and Outline**
Most of the energy present in plants is lost in their conversion to meat. By consuming plants directly, this loss of energy is avoided. Should we all be vegetarians? Prepare to debate this issue as part of a 4-person team. You will be called upon to present either side, so it is important that you prepare an argument for both sides. Work as a team and coordinate your approach.	Why do some food crops require more energy than others? What energy inputs are necessary to bring foods to market? How much energy is lost at each trophic level?
1 Prepare a case for becoming vegetarian. Build your case by using facts and adding emotion. Practice your style on each other.	1 Debates are lots of fun if you present interesting facts. Keep a sense of focus. Date: _____ / 5
2 Prepare a case for eating meat. Since this is the current practice, try to look for reasons why we eat meat. Use a nutritional approach, and focus on the tradition of meat in the diet of many races and cultures.	2 Consult your friends and family. What do they think of eating meat, or of being vegetarian? Get a range of opinions. Ask other teachers. Speak to the Principal. Date: _____ / 5

One step each day, done by Friday...

The Five Day Project

Project 4.2   The Case for Vegetarians

Name:

---

3 Practice Debate
Find a quiet area and practice how you will debate by facing off 2 against 2.

3 Remember to keep your cool.

Date: / 5

4 Debate Day

4 Instructions

Date: / 5

5 Analyze the results of the debate

5 Instructions
As a class you will review and dissect the key arguments presented by both sides.

Date: / 5

Appendix: Laboratory Safety

The Hazards	The Safe Way
In this column is a list of lab safety issues that you will face in this course	**Read this column to find out how to safely handle the laboratory problem.**
Eye Injury is possible from flying fragments of metal, glass or chemicals; from heat or flames; from caustic solutions such as acids or bases.	*Always wear safety glasses* in the laboratory. Never take your glasses off, even if you have finished your experiment. Other students may not have finished theirs. The safety glass symbol indicates exercises in which safety glasses *must* be worn.
Crowding, Pushing and Horseplay increase the likelihood of a serious injury.	*Attend to your work.* Stay at the station you were assigned, so that there is room to work safely. If your teacher finds that your behaviour is a safety hazard, he or she may remove you from the lab. There is no place for behaviours which place others at risk of injury. Not at school, not at home and not at work.
Disorganized and Dirty Working Conditions are a hazard wherever they are found.	*Keep Lab Area Clean.* Clean and put away unused equipment. Tell your teacher about chipped, cracked, damaged or broken equipment. Do not leave anything on the floor, the desktop, the sink, or the cupboards that is not supposed to be there.
Broken Glass happens even to careful scientists.	*Do Not Touch* broken glass with your hands. Tell your teacher. Use a broom to sweep the glass into a dustpan. Dispose of the broken glass in the special container provided. Do not leave it in the regular wastebasket: it could seriously injure a custodian.
Liquid Spills may consist of water, but they may also contain acids, bases, or toxic chemicals. You may not be able to tell the difference.	*Tell your teacher* about any spills immediately. Do not attempt to clean up without teacher instruction. Only if the teacher decides it's safe, use a cloth or paper towels to soak up excess liquid. Wipe the area clean with a damp cloth. Rinse the cloth frequently in fresh water. Wash your hands afterwards.
Solid Spills may consist of highly reactive chemicals. You may not know the specific hazards.	*Tell Your Teacher* about the spill, whether or not you caused it. Your teacher will instruct you on the safe way to handle the problem. In any case, the spill must be cleaned up promptly.

Appendix: Laboratory Safety

Name:
Date:

Open Flames are a frequent hazard. The Bunsen burner is the most likely safety hazard.	***Review Safe Handling of Bunsen Burner*** with your teacher. Be prepared to show how to light, operate and extinguish the burner at any time. Do not attempt to ignite pens, papers, rulers or other things. That kind of behaviour will certainly result in your being put out of the lab.
Fire. Any liquid solid or gaseous fuel burning where you do not want it to burn is a fire.	***Tell the teacher immediately!*** Do not attempt to extinguish the fire with your hands, books, paper towels etc. Do not panic. Move away from the hazard. ***Your teacher is the best judge of the appropriate course of action.***
Hot Metal or Glass cause more burns than any other hazard. There is usually no visible indication that they are hot. Glass in particular causes small, deep burns.	***Let Hot Objects Cool for 10 - 15 Minutes*** before handling. Place all hot objects on a heat resistant pad. You and your partner will know where they are. Approach hot objects cautiously. Touch them at the coolest point first (the base of the retort rod, the bottom of the Bunsen burner or hot plate, the thumb screw of the iron ring). Use dry, not damp, paper towels to handle hot objects.
Hot Liquids such as boiling water or hot oil spread and splash rapidly. They also cling to skin and clothes.	***Let Hot Liquids Cool for 10 - 15 Minutes*** before handling. Do not heat liquids in closed containers. Use hot plates rather than shaky retort rod assemblies. Do not heat more liquid than you need.
Obstructed Passageways prevent you from moving out the way of a spill or a fire.	***Stand at Your Lab Station.*** Do not bring chairs or stools over to sit down. Your chair will prevent others from moving away from a spill or a fire.
Long Hair or Loose Clothing is more likely to become involved in your equipment. It can cause spills and breakage, or catch fire.	***Tie Back Long Hair; Secure Loose Clothing.*** Outerwear in particular must be avoided in the lab situation. Jackets, sweat suits, hoods, etc are too large and awkward for the lab situation. They are also frequently made of materials that are flammable and can melt and stick to the skin in a fire. Avoid using laquer based hair sprays. A curly head of hair with hair spray can burn up completely in seconds.
Unauthorized Experiments can have unintended results.	***Stick to the plan.*** Read instructions very carefully the night before the lab. Ask questions. Do not try experiments "just to see what happens." The dangers are too great.